"We are people called to love God and love others, and Paul Kim informs and equips our understanding of the world's diverse others. He does so with deep respect for both biblical wisdom and psychological science and with winsome conversational prose that invites readers to engage and relate. I highly recommend *Cultural Diversity and Psychology*, both as a text and as a guide to a culturally sensitive faith and life."

—**David G. Myers**, Hope College; coauthor of *Psychology* and *Social Psychology*

"American Christianity has long been slow to reckon with the ways our faith and our culture are entangled. Kim's book takes that entanglement seriously and begins to close the gap in our understanding. And oh, how we need that gap closed! Reckoning with cultural identity, cross-cultural communication, and cultural engagement is central to living faithfully and effectively today."

—**Michelle Reyes**, Wheaton College

"The telos of studying culture and diversity from a Christian perspective is for us to faithfully pursue the greatest commandments—to love God and to love our neighbor. What many don't realize is that our relationship with God, who is transcendent, is fundamentally an intercultural relationship. And the majority of the global family of God now resides in the Global South and similarly does not share the same cultural assumptions as those of us who live in the West. *Cultural Diversity and Psychology: A Christian Engagement* fills a gap in the literature by equipping people of faith to engage in these topics thoughtfully, rigorously, and in dialogue with core Christian commitments."

—**David C. Wang**, Fuller Theological Seminary

"Textbooks used in cross-cultural psychology or cultural diversity courses often provide only brief foundations for understanding spirituality and religion as cultural variables. Paul Kim, however, provides a helpful companion text that takes a deeper look at cultural variables through a Christian lens. Kim provides focused examples to help readers deepen their understandings of key multicultural concepts through a Christian perspective and challenges readers with thought-provoking exercises and reflection questions. Faculty and students looking for a nuanced, integrative approach with relatable examples will appreciate this book as an adjunct to their other course texts."

—**Veola Vazquez**, licensed psychologist and coauthor of *Healing Conversations on Race*

CULTURAL DIVERSITY AND PSYCHOLOGY

A Christian Engagement

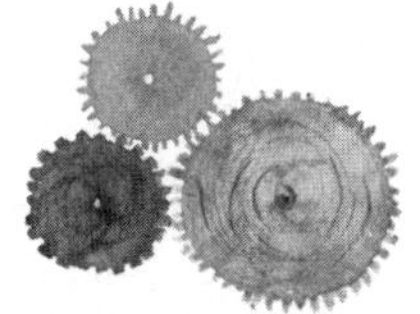

Paul Youngbin Kim

Baker Academic
a division of Baker Publishing Group
Grand Rapids, Michigan

Published by Baker Academic
a division of Baker Publishing Group
Grand Rapids, Michigan
BakerAcademic.com

Printed in the United States of America

Library of Congress Cataloging-in-Publication Data
Names: Kim, Paul Youngbin author
Title: Cultural diversity and psychology : a Christian engagement / Paul Youngbin Kim.
Description: Grand Rapids, Michigan : Baker Academic, a division of Baker Publishing Group, [2026] | Includes bibliographical references and index.
Identifiers: LCCN 2025031057 | ISBN 9781540967565 paper | ISBN 9781540970565 casebound | ISBN 9781493454730 ebook | ISBN 9781493454747 pdf
Subjects: LCSH: Psychology—Religious aspects—Christianity | Cultural pluralism—Religious aspects—Christianity
Classification: LCC BF51 .K47 2026
LC record available at https://lccn.loc.gov/2025031057

Some names and details of the people and situations described in this book have been changed or presented in composite form to ensure the privacy of those with whom the author has worked.

Baker Publishing Group publications use paper produced from sustainable forestry practices and postconsumer waste whenever possible.

26 27 28 29 30 31 32 7 6 5 4 3 2 1

For my mother, who loved to sing
of God's loving-kindness across cultures

Contents

Acknowledgments

I have discovered that writing a book is an arduous endeavor. I am grateful to the people who came alongside me and served as counters to the negative self-talk that kept creeping into my mind. I wish to thank my departmental colleagues at Seattle Pacific University for their communal support. I am especially grateful for the support and flexibility of my department chair, Baine Craft, and dean, Katy Tangenberg. I thank the Office of Sponsored Programs and the Faculty Life Office at Seattle Pacific University for a faculty research grant that opened up additional writing time for me and provided funding for reading materials. I am thankful to Kristen Hoffman for her invaluable support as a librarian.

I want to recognize my amazing undergraduate research students, who provided detailed and helpful feedback that only students can provide on many chapters of this book: Wesley Joo, Rafi Pezo Acosta, Kaley Rodda, and Esal Shakil.

All the guests on my *Teaching Cross-Cultural Psychology* podcast, whether knowingly or unknowingly, shaped my thinking that went into this book: (in order of appearance) Jordan Shannon, Peter Rivera, David Myers, Jessica ChenFeng, Brittany Tausen, David Wang, David A. Tizzard, Marcia Webb, Veola Vazquez, Liz Lin, Raedene Copeland, Michelle R. Loyd-Paige, Marcella Locke,

Simon Howard, Michelle Ami Reyes, Jeanie Chang, David I. Smith, Helen Chung, Becky White, Cedric Stout, Robert Chao Romero, Grace Inae Blum, Kenneth T. Wang, Alex Jun, Jennifer McKinney, Everett Worthington, Loli Kim, Jorge Preciado, Sara Shaban, and Joel Jin.

I wish to thank Don Tellinghuisen for patiently answering my questions about the publication process with Baker Academic. I want to express my gratitude to Bob Hosack at Baker, who reached out to me with encouragement to submit a book proposal, and to the many folks at Baker who worked with me and supported me in writing this book.

I am deeply grateful to my friend and mentor John Hwang, who passed away unexpectedly while I was writing this book. Without his encouragement and guidance, I would not have been able to complete it.

I appreciate the support of my family: my parents, who have had such a strong influence on my Christian faith and how I see cultures and the people who make up those cultures; my sister, Joo Eun, who read every chapter draft and provided detailed feedback; Sarah, my life partner of seventeen years and counting, who put up with me filling our evening walks with my ideas for this book; my daughters, Alyssa and Abigail, who in their own personalities found ways to encourage their father to keep writing; and my dog, Bijou, who was a faithful and patient companion next to me while I clacked away at the keyboard.

Finally, I am deeply thankful for my past and present students in Cross-Cultural Psychology, including those students who have pushed back on the course materials. You challenge me to think more deeply and flexibly about my convictions and how I deliver them.

Introduction

Why and How We Should Study Culture and Psychology in a Christian Faith Perspective

"Why are you enrolled in this class?"

My guess is that you have been asked, and perhaps mildly annoyed by, this question many times during your academic career. At the start of each term in my Cross-Cultural Psychology course, I ask students this basic question on an introductory survey. Some students are refreshingly honest and reply that it is because the class is required for the major; I completely understand this mindset. But some of the other frequent student responses over the years also have been telling: "I want to be a mental health professional and want to work with diverse cultures" and "I want to make myself as competitive as possible for the workplace" are some examples that come to mind. So, among my students, there is shared motivation driven primarily by practical outcomes (e.g., acquisition of skills valuable for a future vocation). And this is a good thing. Consistent with my students' instincts about the worth of studying how culture and psychology relate to each other, the American Psychological Association (APA), in its various guidelines for psychology students, emphasizes the importance of culture, diversity, and inclusion. For example, a document highlighting transferable skills for psychology students identifies inclusivity as a vital interpersonal skill, describing it as a skill that leads one to "demonstrate sensitivity to cultural and individual differences and similarities by working effectively with diverse people, respecting and considering divergent opinions, and showing respect for others."[1]

Less frequently, I get student responses that explicitly articulate a Christian faith perspective as motivation for taking my course. My students tend to be divided on Christian faith integration into studying cultural diversity and psychology. In fact, another question on my introductory survey asks students to rate how important faith integration in the class is to them. In my most recent questionnaire, conducted in the spring of 2025, 13 percent rated faith integration as the lowest priority ("not at all important"); only 4.3 percent rated it as the highest priority ("extremely important"). The rest of the group reported varying levels of importance (30.4 percent said "very important," 34.8 percent said "moderately important," and 17.4 percent said "slightly important").

So, from what I can gather, students are in different places when it comes to the study of culture's relation to psychology in a Christian faith perspective. Some desire lots of faith engagement, some want a moderate amount, and others see little value in it.

In this introduction, I would like to put forward some compelling reasons to study culture and psychology in a Christian perspective. I will then provide some initial thoughts on *how* to go about doing that, including some practical suggestions on how to engage the materials in this book. I will wrap up the introduction by articulating how my own cultures have shaped the materials in this book.

Why Culture, Psychology, and Christian Faith?

Broadly speaking, we must study culture and its relation to psychology in a Christian faith perspective because it can help us

1. Naufel et al., "Skillful Psychology Student," 1.

love our neighbors better, including (and especially) the culturally different neighbors. As you begin reading this book, my prayer is that by the end you will have acquired the knowledge to utilize the tools available in psychology to love across cultural differences. Psychological science demonstrates that it is easier for you and me to love those who are similar to us than those who are different from us (see, e.g., social identity theory, which asserts that we relate to in-group members much more favorably than out-group ones).[2] But Christian love calls us to love our neighbors (Mark 12:31) without qualifications. In the language of this book, we, as learners and appliers of psychology, are called to demonstrate God's love across cultures using the tools available in psychology.

Another reason Christian students must care about the intersection of culture and psychology is that, succinctly put, religion matters. In the language of research methods, various constructs representing Christian faith can facilitate or hinder psychological outcomes; alternatively, these constructs can also moderate an existing empirical association between culture and psychological outcomes.

On the one hand, it is true that Christian faith can hurt. At times, religion can interfere with beneficial psychological outcomes. At various points in this book you will be challenged to grapple with troubling examples of the deleterious role of religion (including Christian faith) and related constructs in the intersection of culture and psychological outcomes. When you and I, as followers of Jesus seeking to faithfully live out the calling to love our neighbors, learn of some of the ways that Christianity can inflict harm, it is an opportunity for genuine self- and communal reflection and, ultimately, repentance.

On the other hand, there are times that Christian faith can help. Again, borrowing the language of research methods, religion is often viewed as a buffer in the stress-distress relation of

2. Tajfel and Turner, "Social Identity Theory," 15–17.

minoritized communities.[3] Taking a step back, this protective feature of religion is a reminder of how faithful communities that love their neighbors can be a light for people in stressful situations. In this book, you will see examples in psychology of how certain aspects of Christian faith can help facilitate human flourishing.

In sum, we study the association between culture and psychology in a Christian faith perspective because it allows us to affirm how Christian faith can help improve human lives across or within cultures. We as Christian communities should keep doing what we are doing—if it is helpful for people. But on the flip side, psychology also should lead us to take a hard look at our own Christian communities and how some aspects of the ways we are living out our faith, intentional or not, are falling short of loving our neighbors as God intended.

Finally, we study psychology, culture, and Christian faith because when we elevate marginalized or decentered stories in psychology (and by extension, elevate marginalized *people*), we are demonstrating a tangible love of our neighbors. On the flip side, when stories are pushed to the margins, we fall short of loving the people who are part of those stories. Allow me to use two personal stories here to make my point.

When I was an undergraduate student majoring in psychology, I conducted an independent research project on attitudes toward counseling among international students in the US. It was my first ever research study, and when an opportunity to present the findings at a regional undergraduate research conference came up, I jumped on it. When I arrived at the conference location, I browsed through the titles and descriptions of the other presentations in the printed program, and it struck me how very few presentations focused on cultural themes. In fact, the conference presentations were grouped according to shared themes, but my presentation seemed only tangentially related to the other projects. That was the first red flag. When it was my turn to present, I

3. P. Kim et al., "Religious Coping Moderates."

was nervous, but I was also eager to communicate the importance of the findings with students and professors. Following my presentation, there was time set aside for interaction with the audience. Given what I observed in the student presentations before mine, I was eager for feedback, affirmation, questions—really, any kind of engagement. To my initial surprise, which quickly turned into dismay, what followed instead was awkward silence and averted eyes. No questions, no feedback. The eager people who clamored to speak up in the other presentations, the same folks who had no trouble filling the Q&A times of the other research projects with thoughts on the implications of the findings and affirmation of the students' work, did not appear to see how my findings on international students also mattered. It was then that I realized how alone I was in that large auditorium. I was (and my presentation was) invited to this physical space, but the message conveyed was that what I had to offer was not equal to the value of the other projects. Given the strong cultural emphasis of my study, I couldn't help but wonder if the study of culture was viewed as secondary or peripheral by the attendees.

My second story begins when I was working at a university counseling center. During a meeting, I proposed doing a presentation for students on racial microaggressions. I was excited to present this topic as a clinical outreach because of my own research interests. I thought that education about the topic, and about ways of coping, might help the student body. After I pitched the idea, a colleague looked at me, paused, and asked somewhat dismissively, "What are microaggressions?" Taken aback by this response, I couldn't formulate a solid answer, and the presentation idea got scratched. Afterward, with my peers, I processed how the colleague's response itself felt like a microaggression, that my passion and expertise for talking about the psychological impact of racism had been invalidated.

I share these two stories to illustrate the costs of the marginalization of certain stories. I share them with you as examples of errors to avoid as a psychology learning community. I should also add that I am grateful my overall journey in psychology has been such that stories like these are the exceptions. I have had many corrective experiences when colleagues and students have supported—*centralized*—the stories I have told through psychology. I will share these examples too. My prayer is that you and I as members of the psychology community always strive to elevate or centralize stories that have been pushed to the edges in psychology; that we would live out the true inclusiveness of Jesus; that we would seek to emulate our God, whose heart is for the brokenhearted (Ps. 34:18); that the glorious vision of every community coming together before God as equals and worshiping him (Rev. 7:9) would be something that can be realized (even if not in full here on this earth) in a tangible way when we honor and center stories that have been previously marginalized.

How Should We Approach Culture, Psychology, and Christian Faith?

With the love of all neighbors as the basis, next I will propose *how* we might implement studying psychology in a Christian perspective. If the overarching goal is the love of all neighbors, I propose that the how of the implementation should be a balancing act. It is, admittedly, a difficult balancing act, but one that faithful Christians looking to improve in loving their neighbors through psychology must be able to do. In this space I would like to propose a few guidelines to keep in mind. When we study how culture, faith, and psychology are intertwined, we must do so with hope, knowledge, humility, and confidence.

With Hope, but Also with Lament

As followers of Jesus, we have genuine hope that all things will be made right. But this hope is not disconnected from the reality of our imperfect world; there is an understanding that we are called to lament the individual and collective suffering that is all around us. It's the paradoxical perspective that gives Christian communities real, unshakable hope and, at the same time, empathy for the cries of individuals and communities near and far. Indeed, the study of culture and psychology tends to be filled with themes that should trouble us (e.g., social injustices, health and mental health disparities, misuse of psychological research). When you encounter these themes, sit with the troubled emotion(s). Lament the consequences of our sinful world on people and the communities that they are a part of, especially the communities that are marginalized and oppressed. And through it all, reflect on how your hope and lament are intertwined and necessary for a proper engagement in the field of psychology.

Every two years I lead a short-term study abroad in South Korea. In this program, ten or so students from my American institution travel with me to Seoul to take Cross-Cultural Psychology against the backdrop of Korean culture. One of the most powerful activities during this study abroad is when they learn about the girls and women who were forcibly taken as sexual slaves during the Japanese colonial period. Every time my students learn about this collective trauma of Korea, I observe them lament, whether through tears that freely flow or other expressions of sadness and anger. But during their grief, I paradoxically feel hope.

Here is what Emi Ichimura (my TA on the program) and I wrote in a *Christian Scholar's Review* blog: "Hope for validation of other experiences that have yet to be shared. Hope for the recognition of pain held inside. Hope for a better world for young girls and women all over the world. Hope for a world where every tear will be wiped away, and that death and crying and sorrow will be gone (Revelation 21:4)."[4] As you read this book, and as you study how culture, psychology, and Christian faith are related, hold on to the hope we have in Jesus. But also, part of that hope is to grieve and to lament the atrocities and injustices that we see in our world and to work to make them right.

4. Ichimura and Kim, "'Hope, but It's a Complex Kind': Part 1."

With Knowledge, but Also with Attitudes and Skills

Whenever psychologists refer to cultural competence, they typically mean a three-pronged understanding of it: knowledge, attitudes, and skills.[5] Now it should not be a surprise that this book will emphasize knowledge the most; it is a book after all. But it should also deepen your understanding of your own cultural identities and the perspectives and biases that arise out of those identities (i.e., attitudes). Yes, it is scary to think about and even name our own biases and assumptions (it is super frightening for me), but I encourage you not to skip out on doing the quick reflections labeled "pause to reflect" throughout the book. Journaling might also be helpful. Reflecting on your attitudes is consistent with the Christian belief that vast knowledge cannot transform unless paired with a heart that is aligned with God. Without reflection, all that knowledge is like "a resounding gong or a clanging cymbal" (1 Cor. 13:1).

Similarly, this book will emphasize knowledge more than skills. This book is not a manual of how to behave properly in cross-cultural settings. However, I do think that some action steps can naturally flow out of the type of attitudinal reflections and knowledge acquisitions that occur through a book like this. I would argue that some action steps are a necessary part of what it means to hope and lament. In part 2 of the *Christian Scholar's Review* blog post that I cited earlier, we wrote about the connection between hope, lament, and action: "Hope is not a passive posture. . . . True hope includes our diligent participation in God's restorative work."[6] My prayer for you as you read this book is that you will see how acquired knowledge and attitudinal change can come together to inspire you to action steps that will help you love your neighbor a little better.

5. D. Sue et al., "Multicultural Counseling Competencies," 481–83.
6. Ichimura and Kim, "'Hope, but It's a Complex Kind': Part 2."

With Humility, but Also with Conviction

Related to the attitudinal aspects of competence from earlier, a posture of humility is needed when studying culture, psychology, and Christian faith. A bidimensional conceptualization of cultural humility is helpful for our purposes: There is an intrapersonal dimension, which is a person's recognition that they have limitations in their capability to understand the worldviews of other people, and there is an interpersonal dimension, which is a way of relating to other people with an intentional focus on them and without a sense of being better than them.[7] As you study culture and its relation to psychology, monitor your intrapersonal and interpersonal aspects of humility. Are you keeping in mind the possibility that you might be wrong in your perspective? Are you checking for any sense of superiority that may creep into your interaction with someone who is from a different cultural background?

Even as I type this next example, I am aware of how my spirit is resistant to the sharing of the story. As a sinful being, my pride gets in the way of disclosing my own shortcomings. But in the spirit of demonstrating vulnerability, here it is.

In a PowerPoint slide describing racial microaggressions, I listed the phrase "alien in one's own land" as a common microaggression, citing a published article.[8] I had used this slide multiple times with my Cross-Cultural Psychology students over the years. But one particular day, a student pointed out that this was dehumanizing terminology and that I should not even make it visible on a PowerPoint slide. She proceeded to share about her family's experience of immigration to the US and how the term "alien" had been weaponized against her and her family members.

Do you know what my initial internal response was? It was one of defensiveness instead of humility. I found myself thinking things like, "But the published literature uses this term." Or, "I have been using this terminology for so long, and no one has

7. Hook and Davis, "Cultural Humility," 72.
8. D. Sue et al., "Racial Microaggressions in Everyday Life," 276.

pointed this out until now." Or, "I am using it as a negative example, not endorsing it, so it is not on me." While these thoughts were jumping around in my head, I also had a counternarrative that nudged me toward a posture of cultural humility. Specifically, I had to remind myself that my understanding of the student's experiences and worldview was limited by my own biases and assumptions. And in my verbal response to the student's comment, I had to practice interpersonal cultural humility so that I did not come across as superior or as having all the answers but instead as deeply honoring her concerns.

But cultural humility does not negate the need for a sense of conviction.[9] At some parts of this book, you might encounter things that you disagree with or at least are uncertain about. In your conversations with other people, you might not see eye to eye. Cultural humility does not mean that personal convictions must be set aside. Instead, articulate your convictions, but always keep in mind the possibility that you might have missed something and that the person in front of you or the contents of this book could help you learn something new about culture, psychology, and Christian faith.

The term "critical lens" might be another way to refer to having a conviction. In a real sense, social scientists like me are trained to critique personal, interpersonal, and cultural dynamics. Professor Alexander Jun recently said on my podcast that "learning to have a critical lens but not a critical spirit" is a delicate balance for Christian scholars, especially those who are in the business of naming and calling out social problems.[10] As you engage in the topics of this book, monitor your spirit and ask yourself this question: Am I utilizing a critical lens right now, or am I feeding into a critical spirit?

With Confidence, but Also with Psychology in Its Proper Place

I encourage you to embrace psychology's ability to answer questions about you and me. In reality, though, Christian communities

9. McConnell et al., "Including Multiculturalism," 10.
10. P. Kim, "Racism and Total (with a Big T) Depravity."

can foster skepticism of the social sciences, especially when cultural diversity is considered.

I was once sitting in a guidance counselor's office, discussing strategies for submitting college applications. At some point in the conversation, I disclosed to her that I was hoping to major in psychology. In response, the counselor looked at me pointedly and proceeded to let me know that if psychology was in fact what I wanted to study, I should consider applying only to Christian colleges and universities. Her reason? Psychology taught in non-Christian settings (and by non-Christian professors) was not to be trusted.

Has anyone expressed similar sentiments to you, stemming from their assumption that psychology and Christianity are not compatible? Perhaps not to the same extreme as my counselor, but I would guess that you have encountered voices that have tried to nudge you away from psychology or have insinuated that it is not to be trusted.

As you continue to read this book, I encourage you to *trust* psychology—not in the sense that psychology is a flawless academic discipline, and certainly not in the sense that psychologists who conduct research have it right all the time. (If you were a fly on the wall for any of my research team meetings, you would see me regularly admitting something to the effect of "I thought this was the case, but now I see that it should be . . .") But I implore you to trust that the findings psychologists are sharing through their empirical research have merit and will help answer the types of questions that psychology has the capability of answering.

In the important book *Psychology and Christianity: Five Views*, five different views of how psychology and Christianity relate to each other are presented and debated.[11] Briefly, the biblical counseling view argues that mainstream psychology is too secular and that only the Scriptures and Christian theology should inform

11. Johnson, *Psychology and Christianity*.

psychology.[12] The Christian psychology view argues for a distinctively Christian perspective in understanding human nature.[13] The integration view holds psychology in high regard, but it is also not shy about bringing in Christian perspectives to understand and at times critique psychology.[14] The levels-of-explanation view argues that there are varying levels of explaining our world and that psychology occupies a particular level that is different from the level of something like theology.[15] Finally, the transformational psychology view asserts that what makes psychology Christian is the understanding that "*how* Christians live out their Christianity in the field of psychology and counseling is at least as important as seeking to understand human beings Christianly."[16]

In this book on how culture, psychology, and Christian faith should connect, I am especially drawn to the levels-of-explanation and integration perspectives. That is, you will see me utilizing psychological studies to draw connections to faithful Christian living without necessarily qualifying or critiquing the use of the Bible or Christian traditions (i.e., levels-of-explanation). You will also see me drawing from Christian perspectives to affirm or critique psychology perspectives (i.e., integration). Put differently, I am of the belief that a faithful engagement of culture and psychology should hold psychology in high regard but at the same time make meaningful connections to Christian faith, whether in affirmation or critique.

Moreover, I believe that a suspicion of psychology and its connection to cultural themes can impede the very thing that Christian learning communities strive to do, which is to find God's truth in all our endeavors. On the flip side, seeing the value of psychological science in God's good work among his people can be an incredibly liberating and joyful experience.

12. Powlison, "Biblical Counseling View."

13. Roberts and Watson, "Christian Psychology View."

14. Jones, "Integration View."

15. Myers, "Levels-of-Explanation View."

16. Johnson, "Brief History," 37; see also Coe and Hall, "Transformational Psychology View."

Remember my story about the counselor telling me I should apply to only Christian colleges? As an "obedient" student, I did just that, and I ended up at Calvin College (now Calvin University) for my undergraduate education. Ironically, Calvin opened up psychology to me in a way that no protectionist mentality could. As an undergraduate student I dove deep into learning about psychology, taking stimulating psychology classes with wonderful Christian professors. At no point did any of my professors imply that a narrow version of "Christian" psychology should be pursued or that psychological science should not be trusted. My narrow view of psychology was broadened, my passion for the subject was deepened, and I loved every minute of it. In college I was inundated with the idea that all things in this world belong to God, including all academic disciplines. Until college I had been told that there needed to be a clear separation of the secular from the Christian. Listening to "non-Christian" music was frowned on, and "evolution" was a forbidden word even in biology classrooms. In contrast, studying psychology as an undergraduate student ignited a passion in me, and I recognized the vocation I chose in psychology as being just as sacred as the vocation of a missionary or a priest. This was a liberating process. Even though I had made up my mind to go into psychology, I realized that I was subconsciously ashamed of my field and had received such messaging from other Christians around me. The transformation that took place in me during college freed me to pursue psychology with a renewed zeal, with the assurance that ultimately God is glorified through my work.

I pray for similar confidence for you as you read this book and learn about culture and psychology in a Christian perspective. I pray that, on the one hand, you will understand that psychology's focus is clearly and narrowly defined: the how and why of behavior, cognition, and emotion. Psychology cannot answer what David Myers and Malcolm Jeeves refer to as "life's ultimate questions."[17]

17. Myers and Jeeves, *Psychology Through the Eyes of Faith*, 11.

On the other hand, I pray that this acceptance of the limits of psychology will free you up to embrace psychological science as a gift from God to be utilized as a tool to make a difference in people's lives. As David Myers aptly writes, "In psychology, we need more Christian scholars not in the stands but down on the playing field."[18]

A Note About My Own Cultural Identities

Finally, I want to briefly share my own personal and professional backgrounds and how they have shaped the contents of this book. Professionally, I am a college professor at a Christian liberal arts institution in the Pacific Northwest (PNW) US. Also, I am trained as a counseling psychologist, and my training emphasized cultural perspectives related to mental health. As such, I feel passionate about the integration of Christian faith and cultural perspectives into all aspects of my teaching. Given my professional roles and passion, I am envisioning that this book will be primarily read by people like my students (and hopefully by my students): undergraduates enrolled in a Christian higher education institution located in the US and taking a psychology class that is intentionally focused on the relation between culture and psychology (e.g., Cross-Cultural Psychology, Multicultural Psychology). Furthermore, because of its purposeful, narrow focus on Christian faith, this book is meant to serve as a *supplement* to more comprehensive textbooks.

In this book you may notice a propensity toward concepts and examples that are especially applicable in the US setting but that also arise from Korean and Asian American cultures. You likely guessed it from my last name—I am of Korean heritage. But in addition to my Korean background, I am also influenced by my "missionary kid" (MK) identity (I grew up in the Philippines as a child of cross-cultural missionaries) and all the cultural correlates

18. Myers, "Steering Between the Extremes," 383.

that come with that identity. My childhood and adolescent years were spent outside the US, but from college on, I have lived in the US and now consider the PNW my home. As we will see in chapter 2, it is important for us to name the personal experiences and perspectives that can shape the work we put forward in psychology.

1

What Are We Talking About?

Defining Culture

> Culture is a fuzzy construct.
>
> —Harry C. Triandis et al., "Individualism and Collectivism"

We talk about "culture" all the time. And as the opening quote of this chapter descriptively and aptly captures, we might mean very different things whenever we bring up the word. Just the other day I talked to a friend about *teen* culture (i.e., the culture of my two daughters). To be candid, I might have complained a bit about their culture. In that conversation, I was applying a definition of "culture"—that is, operationalizing it—as *age* dependent. My children are often described as members of the Gen Z culture, whereas I barely make the cut for the millennial cultural group.

Obviously, age and year of birth are not the only determinants of culture, or even the most important ones in most situations. Even though my daughters and I are a few decades apart (and they remind me of this difference regularly), we also have commonalities when it comes to cultures. All of us identify as Korean

Americans, which means that we share in the cultural aspects of being Korean, American, and Korean American. By extension, we are all people of color in the US. We also share in the culture of Christianity.

This brings me to a couple important points that Hector Betancourt and Steven López make regarding defining and assessing culture in psychology. They write that as long as "cultural research specifies what is meant by culture in terms that are amenable to measurement," it is fine for psychology to embrace different definitions of "culture."[1] Put simply, culture, when studied in psychology, must be measurable. If I propose a definition of "culture" as some kind of unspoken, unconscious energy but am unable to articulate a method for assessing that unconscious energy, then that definition cannot be taken seriously in psychology. The second implication of Betancourt and López's assertion is that it is vital to define "culture" in psychology clearly so that everyone is talking about the same thing. Otherwise, confusion and misunderstanding might result.

In this chapter I will first discuss how psychology's understanding and application of culture can be enhanced by some fundamental truths of Christianity. After that, I will provide an overview of the commonly used methods of defining "culture" and utilizing it in the field of psychology, along with commentaries from a Christian faith perspective.

Pause to Reflect

How do *you* define "culture"? Don't worry about getting it right or coming up with a polished definition. Simply reflect on what elements are essential to thinking about culture. After you come up with some thoughts, pay attention to how what you emphasized maps onto some of the ideas that are presented in this chapter.

1. Betancourt and López, "Study of Culture," 630.

Culture and Core Christian Beliefs

Although a comprehensive theologizing about culture is beyond the scope of this book, it is nonetheless important to highlight how a couple fundamental truths in the Christian tradition can enrich and reinforce social science's conceptualization of culture. Drawing specifically from William Edgar's book *Created and Creating: A Biblical Theology of Culture*, I will discuss three truths in connection to culture: people as image bearers, our fallenness, and the need for critique.

The first truth is that culture is developed by God's image bearers.[2] An implication of this truth is that when we engage in a culture outside of our own, we must approach the endeavor with a deep respect for the image bearers who make up that culture. This simple truth is difficult to practice; as we will see later in this chapter and throughout the book, psychological research tells us that cross-cultural interactions are fraught with judgments and attitudes of superiority.

The second truth is regarding our fallenness. That is, the honoring of other cultures must be held in balance with the notion that "because of the fall, culture can and has become sinister."[3] Of course, it must be recognized that if other cultures can go awry because of sin, so can our own culture(s).

Indeed, the recognition that cultural values and actions can go awry is congruent with the Christian worldview that, because of the reality of sin, people have fallen short of what is acceptable before God (see Rom. 3:23). This deep understanding of our sinful nature as people should logically extend to the idea that *collective* sin—the shortcomings of a group of people or culture—is a reality in our world. In the individualistic worldview of Western Christianity, though, we tend to amplify individual sins at the expense of collective ones. In a clever critique of this imbalance,

2. Edgar, *Created and Creating*, 176.
3. Edgar, *Created and Creating*, 177.

Alexander Jun describes this phenomenon as ignoring the "big T" of "Total Depravity" in the five points of Calvinism (TULIP).[4]

Social psychology has revealed compelling ways consistent with Christian theology that people in groups can misbehave. You might have heard about groupthink, the tendency for individuals in a group setting to be hesitant to go against the opinion of the group for various reasons.[5] Social identity theory argues that people evaluate their own in-group more favorably than outgroups.[6] Translated to the language of "culture," this tendency might mean that people are prone to viewing their own culture as superior or more desirable than others' cultures, which in its extreme form can be described as ethnocentrism.[7] Given our tendency toward groupthink and ethnocentrism, it is no wonder that the Bible writers encourage us to counter these group tendencies by elevating others over ourselves (e.g., Phil. 2:3).

So shortcomings of a cultural group should not surprise us, given the effects of our sins. For example, in this book, more than once we will see how a hyperindividualistic application of the Christian faith can result in a justification of wrongdoing. Michael Emerson and Christian Smith, in their acclaimed book *Divided by Faith: Evangelical Religion and the Problem of Race in America*, describe how the culture of White evangelicals in the US tends to embrace a "cultural tool kit" characterized by three beliefs. First, there is *accountable freewill individualism*, which is a belief that individuals are responsible for any plights that they might find themselves in. Second, the tool kit includes a belief in *relationalism*, which is the tendency to view social problems such as racism as interpersonal; under this perspective, racism becomes all about how you treat me (or how I treat you). Finally, *anti-structuralism* de-emphasizes laws

4. P. Kim, "Racism and Total (with a Big T) Depravity"; Rothwell, "What Is TULIP?"

5. *APA Dictionary of Psychology*, "groupthink," last updated November 15, 2023, https://dictionary.apa.org/groupthink.

6. Tajfel and Turner, "Social Identity Theory of Intergroup Behavior," 15–17.

7. Pettigrew, "Ethnocentrism," 827.

and policies as contributing factors to difficulties that people might experience.[8]

Disconnected from context, the cultural tool kit might sound attractive and even compatible with the tenets of Christian faith. Individual accountability? Interpersonal understanding of sin? These are things that appear to connect to faithful Christian living.

But sometimes this cultural tool kit and other similar frameworks interfere with empathy for the experiences of others who might be suffering due to factors beyond their individual control. Again, later on in this book you will read examples of how this kind of framework can lead to the invalidation of experiences of other cultures, such as the invalidation of structural racism.

Returning to Edgar's discussion, the third truth is that, because of the imperfection of cultures, a Christian worldview calls us to assess cultures and call out any areas of shortcomings. William Edgar writes about culture, "And although value judgements should be made cautiously, they are surely appropriate."[9]

In psychology we are socialized to be tentative in any value judgments, keeping in mind that the tools available to us in the field of psychology tend to be primarily descriptive.[10] But there are times when psychological science does allow for some firm conclusions and applications, especially when paired with a Christian understanding of human flourishing.

You might recall that during the COVID-19 pandemic there was a dramatic increase in the number of hate incidents directed at Asians and Asian Americans.[11] My colleague Brittany Tausen and I decided to empirically examine White college students' awareness of, or *ethnocultural empathy* for, the difficulties of their Asian and Asian American peers during the COVID-19 pandemic.[12] Our

8. Emerson and Smith, *Divided by Faith*, 76.

9. Edgar, *Created and Creating*, 10.

10. Myers and Jeeves, *Psychology Through the Eyes of Faith*, 6–11.

11. Yellow Horse et al., *Stop AAPI Hate*.

12. For more on ethnocultural empathy, see Y. Wang et al., "Scale of Ethnocultural Empathy."

research found that empathy of White students for their Asian American peers was related to how much their peers voiced their concerns about the injustice.[13] In other words, examples of activism set by friends were impactful in increasing ethnocultural empathy. Even though this was a correlational study, Dr. Tausen and I felt comfortable speaking up about the need for more changes in the culture of our participants (i.e., White culture) to include more intentional contact with and exposure to how their peers were engaging in activism. As Christian scholars, we kept in mind the biblical call to "mourn with those who mourn" (Rom. 12:15). If a cultural group of Jesus followers is made aware of a deficit (e.g., a lack of ethnocultural empathy) in relating to a group that is oppressed, then they should take reasonable steps to address that deficit. In this particular research study, then, our critique of the lack of intentional exposure to activism in the culture of our participants was a "value judgment," one that we put forward cautiously, and hopefully hospitably, but also with conviction—as it was something that we felt compelled to do on the basis of Christian principles.

Next I will provide brief overviews of several frameworks for thinking about culture in psychology.

Identity Groups

One way to think about culture is to think about groups that share a culture. Groups share a culture on the basis of country, language, ethnicity, gender, disability, and sexual orientation.[14] I would also add religion, socioeconomic status, and geographic location to that list. If I were to identify my own identity groups for the categories that I just listed, they would be as follows:

Country: South Korea and the United States
Language: English and Korean

13. P. Kim and Tausen, "White College Students' Ethnocultural Empathy," 308.
14. Matsumoto and Juang, *Culture and Psychology*, 17–19.

Ethnicity: Korean, Asian, Korean American, and Asian American
Gender: cisgender male
Disability: able-bodied
Sexual orientation: straight
Religion: Christian
Socioeconomic status: middle class
Geographic location: PNW region of the US

Pause to Reflect

Take a moment to think about *your* responses to the listed categories. Are any of the dimensions difficult to respond to? Easy? What might your ease or difficulty say about the type of cultural socialization, or the lack thereof, that you have experienced?

When it comes to the various identity groups, it is also important to recognize that these groups do not operate in parallel; rather, the groups influence and interact with one another. This notion is referred to as *intersectionality*. Kimberlé Crenshaw is recognized as the scholar who coined the terminology to describe the need to examine racism in relation to gendered experiences.[15] In cultural psychology, gendered racism is an important area of research that examines how some contemporary forms of racism might also reflect gender bias.[16]

We can also think of intersectionality as the interaction between Christianity and one or more identity groups. As for me, my Christian culture intersects with my geographic location of the PNW region of the US. A readily observable example is that PNW folks are devoted coffee drinkers. (Many of my Seattle friends proudly wear the label of "coffee snob.") Every Sunday, when I look around during worship, I can usually pick out several people

15. Crenshaw, "Mapping the Margins."
16. Williams and Lewis, "Gendered Racial Microaggressions," 368–80.

sipping coffee, something I did not see when worshiping in other parts of the world; in fact, when I was growing up, I was taught it was unholy to eat or drink during service. In contrast, my current church even has a coffee stand in the lobby where churchgoers can come and fill and refill their coffee cups before, during, and after worship.

The coffee example is a rather innocuous example of intersectionality. But what if multiple identity groups coming together results in an unfavorable outcome with a real impact on people? Later on in this book, you will see an example of how racism and Christian culture can come together to influence experiences and perceptions.

Subjective or Objective Culture

Another way to conceptualize culture is to think about the distinction between *subjective* and *objective* cultures.[17] Objective culture includes physical things, such as the food that you prefer, the buildings that you occupy, the narrowness of your roads, and so on. In contrast, subjective culture consists of elements that are internalized and shared among a group of people, such as beliefs, attitudes, values, and practices. These components might be a bit more difficult to identify and describe than aspects of objective culture. If it is not already obvious, psychologists are primarily interested in studying subjective culture.

My former students and I once conducted a research study illustrating both objective and subjective cultural elements: We examined the psychological implications of depicting Jesus as a White or non-White person. Have you ever paid attention to the images of Jesus used in your church materials (e.g., in sermon illustrations or printed bulletins)? More pointedly, have you ever noticed if Jesus is portrayed as a White or non-White person?

17. Triandis, *Analysis of Subjective Culture*; also see Matsumoto and Juang, *Culture and Psychology*, 21–27.

Next time you are at church or browsing through your church website or social media, see if you can pick up on how Jesus is depicted.

Images of Jesus are an objective element of culture—they are physical things (e.g., photos). In contrast, the main findings of our study related to subjective aspects of culture. For instance, although our sample of Asian American college students studying at a Christian university tended to recognize on "paper" (more accurately, on an electronic survey) that Jesus was a non-White person, they nonetheless favored White Jesus images over non-White ones; they were quicker to link positive words with White Jesus than with non-White Jesus, and vice versa for the negative descriptors. This tendency was especially true for those students who claimed that they were neutral and unbiased when they engaged topics related to race. There is so much more to say about the study findings, but for now, let's bring it back to defining "culture"—the study was an apt illustration of objective and (especially) subjective elements of culture.[18]

Pause to Reflect

Take a few moments to think about an identity group that you belong to. Can you list some aspects of your culture that are objective? What about subjective aspects? Which aspects were easier to list for you, and why might that be?

Culture as Multidimensional, Shared, and Relatively Permanent

Despite the different definitions of "culture" that exist in psychology, some commonalities tend to be emphasized in defining it. These commonalities are illustrated in this particular definition

18. P. Kim et al., "Beliefs About Jesus's Race," 333–51.

from Jeffery Scott Mio, Lori A. Barker, Melanie M. Domenech Rodríguez, and John Gonzalez: "The values, beliefs, and practices of a group of people, shared through symbols and passed down from generation to generation."[19]

Three essential aspects of culture are contained in this definition. First, culture includes multiple dimensions or domains, such as "values, beliefs, and practices." In everyday life, we often discuss culture as if it were *solely* behavior or action. What music do people listen to? What food do they eat most often? Which language(s) do they speak? In contrast, a fuller understanding of culture includes a consideration of internal aspects, such as values and beliefs. I will return to this important idea of multiple domains in chapter 6.

Second, culture is shared among a group of people. Think about it. If you were to create a culture but were the lone member of the cultural group, then you would not have really started a culture. A community of people is needed. And how do the people within such a community share a culture? As the definition notes, through *symbols* that represent their culture.

Third, culture is relatively long-lasting. It is transmitted from one generation to the next. So a culture that does not include transmission and is short-lived (e.g., pop culture) is different from the type of culture that psychologists and other social scientists are interested in studying. If you identify as a Swiftie (a diehard fan of Taylor Swift), I hate to break it to you, but that pop cultural identification is not the type of "long-lasting" culture that psychologists are interested in studying.

Let me provide several examples of what these three elements of culture might look like when they come together. First, let's focus on the behavioral versus values/beliefs distinction. In the Christian faith context, the behavioral aspects of religion are emphasized and readily identifiable. Everett Worthington and his coauthors created a measure called the Religious Commitment Inventory-10

19. Mio et al., *Multicultural Psychology*, 8.

(RCI-10), which captures an individual's participation in religion. The RCI-10 asks about behavioral aspects of religious culture, such as engagement in faith literature and giving money to the church.[20]

Internal aspects of religion are also studied extensively in psychology. I want to briefly highlight one aspect of religion that has been influential in my own research: religious coping. Kenneth Pargament, Margaret Feuille, and Donna Burdzy argue that people of faith can utilize religion to cope with life's difficulties in several different ways. They can trust God, but they can also doubt God. They can utilize their faith to make meaning of their situation, or they can despair that their situation is God punishing them.[21] Whatever the type, many aspects of religious coping focus (but not exclusively) on beliefs and values that may not be externally visible.

Similarly, a measure of religiosity, the Duke Religious Index, assesses religion with external measures (e.g., attendance in religious meetings) and internal ones (e.g., subjective spiritual experience).[22] Both are important aspects of Christian culture.

Certain *values* might also be associated with the Christian faith. The Faith at Work Scale includes questions about the meaningful application of religion at work, such as the perception of one's skills as a God-given gift.[23] Again, this perception is an internal aspect of religion but still very important.

Pause to Reflect

Can you think of other examples of values and beliefs that contribute to or help define Christian culture?

20. Worthington et al., "Religious Commitment Inventory," 84–96.
21. Pargament et al., "Brief RCOPE," 52–56.
22. Koenig et al., "Religion Index," 885–86.
23. Lynn et al., "Faith at Work Scale," 236.

Second, the fact that culture is shared by a group of people and transmitted over time is consistent with Christianity's emphasis that faith should not be practiced in solitude. Indeed, the Bible is full of reminders that relational connection to other people is a necessity of the Christian faith. There is a call for believers to be "like-minded" (Phil. 2:2). Passages exhort believers to a life that is harmonious with one another (e.g., Rom. 12:6; 15:5). These passages and many more reflect the importance of believers being in a relationship with one another through shared beliefs and actions.

And third, symbols exist to represent Christian culture. The most obvious symbols are actual drawings and objects that are associated with Christianity. During a recent study abroad to South Korea, one of my American students told me that she was looking for a crucifix to give a family member back home in the US. Despite my initial worry that she would not be able to find what she was looking for, the student eventually found a crucifix in a bookstore of a large cathedral in Seoul; this symbol of Christian faith was something that transcended national boundaries.

But more than literal objects represent Christian culture. In fact, our Christian tradition makes it clear that beyond things like the crucifix, certain actions can represent—symbolize—Christianity. "To act justly and to love mercy and to walk humbly with your God" might be such a "symbol" of following Christ (Mic. 6:8). Taking care of the marginalized (James 1:27) might be another powerful representation of Christian faith.

To reiterate, the ideal understanding of culture includes seeing it as (1) both internal and external, (2) communally experienced and expressed through meaningful symbols, and (3) taught and absorbed across multiple generations. The practice of *seh bae* in the Korean culture is a great illustration of all three aspects. Seh bae is a practice of bowing—not a half bow but a full bow that involves the upper body going all the way down to the floor—during every major holiday, such as New Year's Day. It is typically the children who bow to those who are older. The children wear colorful *hanbok* (traditional Korean clothing) when they bow. In return, the recipient of the bow gives words of blessing and affirmation accompanied by a cash gift. Seh bae and all the associated elements certainly comprise specific actions or behaviors. But underlying this practice are the cultural values of respect for the elderly and of the older generation's responsibility to take care of the younger folks in return. Moreover, the bow itself is a symbol, but so are the literal symbols drawn on the *hanbok* that children wear, symbols that stand for things like good health, wealth, long life, and so on. The colors can also represent different aspects of Korean culture (e.g., social hierarchy). Finally, seh bae is a cultural practice that my wife and I, as Korean Americans, learned from our parents when we were growing up. Furthermore, we teach our own children how to seh bae, and they participate in this ritual every major holiday. So far, they tell us that they will also pass on the tradition to any future children.

Pause to Reflect

Choose one cultural identity. Think about the practices, values, and beliefs that make up that cultural identity. How are they shared among a group of people? What are the symbols? And is there intentional transmission across generations?

Sources of Culture

Yet another way to think about culture is to focus on the *sources* of culture. David Matsumoto and Linda Juang argue that we can think of culture as originating from various domains: group life, environments, resources, and the evolved human mind.[24] Briefly, group life is the notion that there are some key advantages to living

24. Matsumoto and Juang, *Culture and Psychology*, 8–13.

as a group (e.g., being able to share the burden of work). Environments include aspects such as what your land looks like in shaping cultural practices. For example, here in my hometown of Seattle, there is a culture of not going out during the rainy season—we informally refer to it as our hibernation period. The category of "resources" refers to how lack or abundance of materials can directly lead to some cultural practices and values. Finally, the "evolved human mind" refers to how human beings are born into this world with predispositions that will help with survival, such as the social need to connect with other people.

Out of this list, I want to circle back to resources as a determinant of culture and connect this to Christian faith. Matsumoto and Juang write that, in general, lacking resources can lead to a culture of dependence, whereas having plenty can naturally lead to more independence.[25] This makes sense. When nothing is lacking, there is no need for dependency on others; when there is a dire need, turning to others for help is an important survival skill.

When my father was a baby, his mother was older than the typical mother of a baby, and as such, she did not have the physical ability to breastfeed him. I should add that my father's family was poor, which meant that the purchase of baby formula was not an option. My father's life was at real risk because there was no one in the family to feed him.

Can you guess what ended up happening? His mother went door to door in her village, pleading with nursing mothers for their help. And many women stepped in to breastfeed my father. It took a literal village to keep my father alive.

Here is my father, in his own words, capturing the power of interdependence in dire circumstances: "We had little, but our hearts were rich. We were lacking in resources, but the generosity and kindness overflowed. Whenever I returned to my hometown as an adult, I would hear from the older women in the village, 'I nursed you when you were a baby.' Initially, these moments were

25. Matsumoto and Juang, *Culture and Psychology*, 10–11.

awkward, and I was embarrassed; but eventually I came to cherish these moments when I could be reminded of the beauty of human connection and care."[26]

This book features multiple references to the Christian emphasis on our connectedness to one another. Acts 4:32 describes the early church in this way: "All the believers were one in heart and mind. No one claimed that any of their possessions was their own, but they shared everything they had." This type of selflessness, in a real way, was out of necessity—remember, lack of resources means having to depend on others—and it achieved what it intended to achieve. Verse 34 declares "that there were no needy persons among them." Similarly, the connection between resources and dependence on one another is captured in the commandment in Leviticus 23:22: "When you reap the harvest of your land, do not reap to the very edges of your field or gather the gleanings of your harvest. Leave them for the poor and for the foreigner residing among you." Again, this is a picture of how people who need resources can directly benefit from those who have them in the first place.

Key Takeaways

1. When discussing culture in psychology, it is important to be precise in articulating what kind of culture you are referring to.
2. Understanding key truths in Christianity (e.g., the sinfulness of people) can enrich psychology's engagement of culture and related constructs.
3. Cultural identity groups can help us name the groups that we belong to. Intersectionality should also be considered when identity groups are discussed.

26. Tae Hyun Kim, online communication to author, October 18, 2024.

4. "Subjective culture" refers to beliefs and values, whereas "objective culture" refers to physical aspects of culture.
5. Religion as a culture is long-lasting, encompasses internal and external components, and is shared among many people using symbols.
6. Not having much (or anything at all) can translate to a culture of dependence on others.

Activities and Discussion Questions

1. Browse through other published definitions of "culture." Textbooks in multicultural, cross-cultural, and cultural psychology are good sources for this exercise. What do you notice about these definitions in terms of their similarities? Do any key differences strike you? How might you critique the definitions from a Christian faith perspective?
2. Does one have the freedom to *choose* a culture? Why or why not? What is the role of other people in cultural identification? That is, is cultural identification legitimate only if others ascribe it to you?
3. How does your environment (e.g., ecology) shape your culture? What about resources?
4. Think about *one* of your identity groups. How does your group/culture illustrate the reality of our fallenness? How does it exemplify the image of God?

Case Study

Brenda grew up as a child of American missionary parents. Her parents were cross-cultural missionaries in Botswana, but outside of short visits, she did not spend a significant amount of time in the country. Instead, her parents enrolled her in a boarding school for foreign students in Germany, where she studied for over ten years. During her school years Brenda was surrounded by peers from all over the world; many (but not all) of them also identified as missionary kids. After she graduated from high school, she was accepted to a Christian liberal arts institution located in Florida. Because her parents were originally from Florida, and many of their extended family still lived there, Brenda and her parents agreed that this college would be a good fit for her. But Brenda's adjustment to the US/Florida was challenging. Even though on paper she was an American citizen, American values, beliefs, and practices felt unfamiliar to her. Indeed, learning to live in the US felt like learning a whole new language. In one of her classes, as part of a first-day-of-class introduction, the professor asked each student to quickly share where they were from. Brenda felt a familiar sinking sensation in her stomach as her classmates began sharing their responses. How were her classmates able to answer this complex question so easily and so quickly? As her turn approached, Brenda felt her mind going blank, and she ran out of the classroom with tears filling her eyes.

1. How would you describe Brenda's cultural background? How does the concept of intersectionality help you understand the complexity of Brenda's cultural experiences?
2. If you were Brenda's professor and you were made aware of how your introductory question triggered a distressing response, how might you go about addressing this with Brenda? What if you were a classmate who became aware of Brenda's response? A friend?
3. How does the understanding of culture as multidimensional, shared among a group of people, and long-lasting help you comprehend Brenda's experiences? How about culture as subjective versus objective? What about culture being shaped by resources you may or may not have?
4. How can Christian perspectives help someone like Brenda who is experiencing cultural adjustment?

2

Examining Our Hearts as Researchers

Issues in Cross-Cultural Research

When Jeremy was growing up, he attended a small evangelical church located in the Midwest US. Each summer during his high school years, his church would send a youth group out to do short-term missions in a different country. The mission team would travel to these countries and do mission work for about one week and return home. As a college student, when learning about the field of cross-cultural psychology, he thought that much of what was involved in cross-cultural research seemed like doing mission work: traveling to a different country (or connecting with a different culture), collecting data, and then "returning home" to analyze the data.

"Why do I need to learn how to do research if I plan on becoming a therapist?"

The above question is one that my students ask me often, especially when they are just starting out in the psychology major. Take a few moments to see if you can articulate a response to this question. Thankfully, students quickly discover the answer as they progress in their undergraduate training in psychology. Research is the backbone of any application of psychology. Without it, no legitimate practice or application of psychology is possible.

Moreover, research in culture and psychology presents its own methodological and ethical considerations, especially when it comes to working with vulnerable or marginalized groups. In its ethics codes, the APA says that psychologists must adhere to five aspirational principles when conducting psychological research or applying psychology: (1) avoid doing harm (beneficence and non-maleficence), (2) develop trusting relationships with others and practice accountability (fidelity and responsibility), (3) be truthful in all professional endeavors (integrity), (4) avoid unjust practices (justice), and (5) honor people and their cultures (respect for people's rights and dignity).[1] In addition to the broad umbrella of the aspirational principles, the APA has also published specific ethics codes for conducting research with diverse populations. "APA's Guidelines on Race and Ethnicity in Psychology," for example, provides key guidelines related to working with racial and ethnic groups in psychological research.[2] For students who are interested in psychology, both documents are must-reads and available online.

In this chapter, I will first summarize some of the potential problems or concerns that arise when conducting cultural psychology research. Following that, I will discuss how the Christian virtue of humility can serve as a corrective, intrapersonal motivation that can help us align our hearts as we conduct and engage research in culture and psychology.

Concern 1: Lack of Representation

At the most foundational level, the lack of representation is a methodological concern in psychological science. Specifically, the lack of *diverse sampling* in research studies is something that

1. "Ethical Principles of Psychologists and Code of Conduct," American Psychological Association, 2017, https://www.apa.org/ethics/code.

2. APA Task Force, "APA Guidelines on Race and Ethnicity in Psychology," 27–33.

continues to trouble psychology as a discipline. A recent review included an analysis of six flagship journals of the APA published between 2014 and 2018, and it reported that 62 percent of the research samples in those journals were American samples.[3] Furthermore, among those six journals in the same time period, only 15 percent of the research samples in the US were predominantly non-White.[4] Taken together, these findings reveal that what is considered mainstream research in psychology remains *American* in the global context and *White* within the US.

Have you ever utilized a population cartogram? It is a type of map based on population instead of land size.[5] Try googling "population cartogram." Observe how the map differs from what you might be used to seeing on a typical map. For example, the US and Canada—countries with some of the largest lands in the world—will look unmistakably smaller if represented according to population size. What other countries on this map stand out to you?

This quick map exercise is a good reminder of God's heart for the people across the globe. I would guess it is not a controversial statement to say that God cares *equally* about individuals; that is, before God, one person is not more or less valuable than another person. And if that's the case, then psychology's underrepresentation of overrepresented people in the world, and its overrepresentation of underrepresented people (e.g., Americans), is inconsistent with God's heart for individuals. Psychology that claims to help all people should address the needs of all people, and the starting point of that is representation in the participants who make up the study samples.

Concern 2: Beyond Representation

But to be clear, representation is not the only thing, or even the main thing. Even when representation is in place, whenever we

3. Thalmayer et al., "Neglected 95% Revisited," 121.
4. Thalmayer et al., "Neglected 95% Revisited," 123.
5. See Roser, "Map We Need."

encounter psychological research studies that target a particular cultural group, several additional considerations need to be raised. First, we need to question *why* the researchers did so in the first place. This question should not only be asked as an overarching principle to describe one's reasons for entering a profession or field but also be repeated every time we conceptualize and design a research study in psychology. This is why psychology professors emphasize the introduction sections of research papers as much as they do; the introduction tells the reader why the author decided to do what they did. To this point, it is imperative that "researchers identify a clear *theoretical justification* for inclusion of any study population . . . based on knowledge of the relevant cultural and/or environmental context."[6]

Second, there is the issue of trust of researchers. Have you ever had a stranger come by your home? Were you skeptical of them? Most psychologists and psychology students are not literally knocking on doors when they do research, but they do encounter a fair share of distrust whenever they try to recruit participants for research studies. That suspicion amplifies whenever researchers try to recruit participants across cultures. Being unfamiliar with the researchers, being overwhelmed by the amount of information in documents like the research consent form, and feeling like their cultural group has been taken advantage of in the past are all examples of factors contributing to the distrust of psychological researchers and can ultimately lead to difficulty in recruiting diverse participants.[7] Similarly, others have noted that a message of deficit can be conveyed, one that assumes that the minoritized group is substandard compared to the majority group.[8]

Third and closely related, the power differentials between researchers and participants should always be checked. For example,

6. Broesch et al., "Navigating Cross-Cultural Research," 2 (italics original).

7. Gallagher-Thompson et al., "Effective Recruitment Strategies," 488; Chen et al., "Engaging Asian Americans for Mental Health Research," 114; Meinert, "Bridging the Gap," 22.

8. Roosa et al., "Research with Underresearched Populations," 103.

in-group members can consider out-group members to be threatening due to differences in power and resources.[9] As such, cross-cultural researchers can often come across as scary and untrustworthy. As we will see in just a bit, this feeling might be exacerbated in situations where the researchers take on the posture "I am right, and you are wrong. I will give you the answers that you need to improve your lives."

Fourth, comparison studies can be problematic. One might argue that such studies (e.g., Are people from country X happier than people from country Y?) offer a decent starting point in addressing the issue of representation in psychological studies. After all, if studies that are focused on majority groups (e.g., European Americans in the US) are overrepresented, a researcher might justify the inclusion of multiple comparison groups as a logical contribution in the literature. For example, the stigma of mental health counseling was examined across ten different countries in a large-scale study. Both the stigma held by the public and the stigma that is internalized by the individual were measured.[10] An interesting finding (there were many) that emerged from this study was that, compared to the US participants, Brazilian participants reported lower public stigma and internalized stigma.[11] So a clear strength of the comparative methodology is the ability to include multiple groups and also draw conclusions regarding how one group fares against another.

But a potential downside of this comparative method, especially if the authors do not provide a clear justification for why the comparison is needed, is the implied or even explicit elevation of one group over the other. It is what Broesch and coauthors call "West versus rest" methodology.[12] Similarly, Matsumoto and Jones argue that sometimes cross-cultural research findings can be used to stereotype cultural groups in a way that might not

9. Broesch et al., "Navigating Cross-Cultural Research," 3.
10. Vogel et al., "Stigma of Seeking Psychological Services," 175–77.
11. Vogel et al., "Stigma of Seeking Psychological Services," 176.
12. Broesch et al., "Navigating Cross-Cultural Research," 2.

be accurate, and comparisons without theoretical justification certainly have the potential for doing that.[13] This is especially true if there is an empirical finding related to a socially desirable trait. Take introversion and extroversion scores, for example. A cross-cultural comparison of Asian American men and European American men found that European American men were more elevated in their extraversion scores than Asian American men.[14] But to draw a definite conclusion about culture on the basis of this particular result could lead to strengthening existing stereotypes about Asian Americans. It is important to understand that when psychologists talk about cultural differences, they are making a statement based on averages, and there will always be deviations from those averages.

Moreover, a problematic motivation for cultural research is one that is based on superiority, one that basically says that I have (or you have) the better answer. Paul Kivel, when writing about what people of color would appreciate or expect from their allies, points to sentiments like avoiding coming across as the expert on a culture and its experiences or as someone who has the full knowledge of what is good for another person.[15] These thoughts about how allyship can go wrong can also be extended and applied to conversations about how researchers can easily enter this mindset of superiority when working across cultures. In chapter 8 we will dive more deeply into how the mentality of acknowledging but then blaming disparity on minoritized communities is a well-intentioned but problematic component of relating to other communities.

By the way, if you grew up (like I did) in a church that regularly sent its members on short-term mission trips across the globe, these ideas that I am discussing here might sound vaguely familiar. Reread the opening vignette. Can you see the parallels? In the Christian context, the history of cross-cultural missions is filled

13. Matsumoto and Leong Jones, "Ethical Issues in Cross-Cultural Psychology," 324.
14. Eap et al., "Culture and Personality," 637.
15. Kivel, *Uprooting Racism*, 135.

with examples of a colonial mentality—whether explicit or subtle. As Howell writes, "Oftentimes a conversion to Christianity was tantamount to conversion to a European culture's expression of faith and practice."[16] Similarly, in cultural psychology, researchers must monitor their own assumptions about culture and recognize how they can perpetuate a message of deficit or inferiority regarding the cultures that they study.

Motivation for Research

The existing literature highlights numerous ways that cross-cultural researchers can address the issues named above. For example, to ensure that translated measures are equivalent, Brislin's back-translation approach is the standard.[17] If you come across empirical studies that use a translated measure, be on the lookout for some kind of a description of how they ensured the validity of the measure being translated. Likewise, when Stanley Sue critiqued the imbalance between emphasis on empirical rigor and generalizability of research findings, he also proposed several concrete antidotes for the field (e.g., intentional recruitment of minoritized participants in studies).[18] In response to participants' distrust of researchers, especially participants who have trouble trusting someone who is an out-group member, the logical solution seems to be for research teams to be intentional about maintaining a high standard for the cultural competence of the team members interacting with participants.[19] These solutions (and others like them) are crucial for us to keep in mind, regardless of whether we identify as Christian.

But I'd like to take a step back and discuss an overarching principle that might not be emphasized as strongly as concrete

16. Howell, "From 'Selves' to 'One Another,'" 182.

17. Brislin, "Back-Translation for Cross-Cultural Research."

18. S. Sue, "Science, Ethnicity, and Bias," 1072–76.

19. For more ideas related to recruitment of communities of color for research, see Roosa et al., "Research with Underresearched Populations," 102–6.

behavioral antidotes: the *examination of our hearts* when conducting cultural research. One of my family's favorite verses discusses the relevance of our hearts' preoccupations: "May these words of my mouth and this meditation of my heart be pleasing in your sight, LORD, my Rock and my Redeemer" (Ps. 19:14). Applied to the research setting, which is an external endeavor involving concrete outcomes (e.g., data collection), the heart matters because of the need to examine the motivation underlying the research. As such, the intrapersonal aspects of motivation for a research study should be identified and monitored. This is consistent with the biblical wisdom that what lies inside the heart will eventually emerge (Luke 6:45). Likewise, Proverbs 21:2 speaks to God's emphasis on the heart. And the purity of the heart is something that will allow us to see who God is (Matt. 5:8). It seems to me, then, that Christians conducting psychological research must examine and reexamine their hearts' motivations for doing their research and apply corrective measures as needed so that their motivations are not misaligned.

As we saw earlier, the concerns regarding the power differential between researchers and participants, the misuse of the research findings (e.g., reinforcing an existing stereotype), and the deficit perspective are examples of how a heart's desire can go wrong. I would add that these issues, if not addressed, can lead to other concerns, such as distrust. For example, if I see that the research I participated in is being used to reinforce a negative generalization about my culture, then I will be less inclined to trust psychological researchers.

I propose *humility* as an overarching principle. But as easy as it might be to point to this virtue as important in doing research, when the rubber meets the road, a humble posture does come at a cost. Let me illustrate what I mean by "cost" with a story from a mentor whom I deeply respect. This mentor is an accomplished scholar who regularly conducts research about the psychological experiences of a refugee group residing in the Midwest US. Given the lack of existing empirical literature on this population, combined with the mental health risks associated with their experiences of displacement, it would be easy for researchers to contact this community with the message "We have the psychological tools that you need. Let us help you implement those things, for your benefit." The research team might even assert that psychological data must be collected as quickly as possible. In contrast, my mentor and his research team take their time, connecting with the community and then eventually collecting data. My mentor goes to community events, and he participates in things like playing volleyball. (I know for a fact that he does not particularly enjoy playing volleyball.) He might repeat these visits, even though they have no direct connection to the empirical questions he eventually wants to ask. The hours and effort involved in making these connections are the costs.

But I would argue that the rewards are worth it. This humble posture is an antidote to things like the superiority complex that can infest our hearts as researchers. When intentional, genuine human contact is made, the distance between the researcher and the participant is reduced. ("That's the same guy who played volleyball with us!" might be a response when my mentor eventually introduces the research study.) It reminds me of the biblical principle "I have become all things to all people" (1 Cor. 9:22). Moreover, I can also see how a humble, relational posture can benefit the research questions directly: Through the community visits and the conversations that take place, the researchers might gain valuable insight into the stories and experiences of the community that might not have been possible if they were to send a link to a survey. Finally, instead of comparing the experiences of the cultural group against an established standard, the researchers might take a deep dive into the narratives of the people and tell their stories without any attempt to qualify. The stories that would emerge would be that much richer and honor the people who are made in God's image and have not yet had as much of a chance to let their stories be known to the world.

I have two more points to make about humility. First, a humble posture requires the researchers to be honest with their own experiences and biases. Many psychology journals, especially those that publish qualitative studies, require the authors to include a positionality statement, which essentially describes the aspects of the author's backgrounds and experiences that might influence the author's analysis of the data.[20] Whenever I have written such a statement, it has been a humbling experience to recognize my own biases and to articulate them for others. Here is an example of a positionality statement I wrote in an article that focused on the experiences of international students:

> The first author of the study is a faculty member teaching at a Christian liberal arts institution. As a former international student who wrote his dissertation on the topic of international student social support and mental health, he is passionate about capturing the rich experiences of international students, especially in the context of Christian higher education. He has also published extensively in the area of racism and mental health with U.S. samples. Therefore, there might have been potential biases to prematurely look for themes that connect to his research interests of racism and Christian higher education.[21]

Pause to Reflect

Draft your own positionality statement. It might help to first think about a research study in culture, psychology, and Christian faith that you might conduct soon or have conducted in the past. How does the articulation of your own experiences and potential biases help you stay humble?

A final point related to the posture of humility: It is important to give back to the communities that you as a researcher have collected data from. Otherwise, research becomes a form

20. Hamby, "Know Thyself."
21. P. Kim et al., "Racialized Experiences and Perspectives," 7.

of extraction, a colonialism of sorts in empirical research.[22] That is, even if the research process (or publication process) does not require it, it is important that the researcher circles back to the community and offers something beneficial.

When I was a graduate student, my research lab studied the cultural correlates of attitudes toward mental illness among Korean American Christians. A challenge with our research project was that there were very few Korean American Christians (and Christian churches) nearby (an online survey was not an option then). As such, just to collect data, we had to drive four to six hours round trip to Chicago to administer surveys in Korean American churches. Furthermore, the whole process required not only data collection trips but also separate trips to introduce our study and establish relationships. (Remember the volleyball example earlier? We were not playing volleyball, but we certainly were not collecting data.) Eventually, after we were able to collect survey data with a sufficiently large sample, I remember thinking to myself, "Finally! I do not want to do the arduous drive again." But my PhD mentor declared that we would return to the churches to give back to these communities, even if our publication process did not require us to do it. True to her word, we ended up preparing a workshop related to Korean American mental health that we delivered at a Korean church in Chicago. To this day, I remember this lesson in the value of looking after the community through extra efforts like a relevant workshop. We as followers of Christ are sometimes called to the "narrow" road—one that might not be efficient or cost-effective or serve our individual interests directly but that benefits the communities connected to us.

Final Thought: Public-Facing Work as a Christian Calling

John Hwang, my late friend and mentor, devoted his career to coaching Christian scholars like me to transform research content into

22. Broesch et al., "Navigating Cross-Cultural Research," 3.

something more digestible by the larger Christian community. His *The Public Scholarship Manifesto* served as a (right kind of) jolt to Christian academics when it was published, providing an unapologetic argument for why Christian academics and higher education institutions were falling short in reaching the general public with their content and how academics should be more intentional in disseminating their findings. The entire statement—there are ten proclamations with accompanying explanations—is worth a read (and rereads) for those in psychology, but one proclamation in particular jumped off the page for me: "We will behave like a media company."[23]

I don't know about you, but as someone who is trained in traditional academic methods, whenever I encounter the phrase "media company," my mental associations are not necessarily positive. Was John suggesting that we academics turn something sacred to us (i.e., our academic work) into content that might be described as watered down, compromised, and so on?

But a closer read of the proclamation reveals what John meant by the benefits of emulating a media company: "Great work in your guild alone is not enough to face the adaptive challenges and the disruption that higher education is facing. An effective distribution allow[s] you to engage with your audience whenever you want." And again: "The key to building an audience is consistency. . . . They need to hear from you on a regular schedule."[24]

So it seems to me that behaving like a "media company" boils down to consistent and frequent distribution of research information to a target audience. Put differently, this type of consistency and regularity in dissemination requires *extra* discipline on my part (and on your part); it is, in a real way, easier to stick to the academic schedule of publishing and presenting once in a while. But John's words are an important reminder of how we can faithfully

23. Hwang, *Public Scholarship Manifesto*, 8.
24. Hwang, *Public Scholarship Manifesto*, 8–9.

serve others through our scholarship: by being purposeful in letting others know about what is good and helpful and by using methods understandable by those outside academia.

I wanted to share John's wisdom as an encouragement to you. Of course, you should learn about the ways of research, including cultural research—this content is something that should not be compromised in your learning and experiences. But beyond learning of the research content, also be strategic in how you engage and disseminate the research.

Pause to Reflect

You are probably much better than I at utilizing social media to share content widely. How might such platforms allow you to engage and share content related to cultural psychology in a way that contributes to God's good work for human flourishing in this world? And what barriers might you face as you participate in this calling to reach a wider audience for the sake of God's kingdom?

As for me, one significant barrier to "putting myself out there" is myself: my cultural influences, my own insecurities, my misguided belief about humility. (It does not seem humble to promote my research on social media!) But I am grateful to God for some of the reframes to these cognitive barriers. I wrote about this in a *Christian Scholar's Review* blog. I hope that some of these sentiments can resonate with you as you also think about how a more public-facing scholarship can be part of God's faithful work:

> But one counter narrative that has been helpful for me is to remind myself of another important Christian virtue—service to others. Public-facing work has allowed me to serve other people in a way that my peer-reviewed work has not. And service to others (1 Peter 4:10)—as a way to love my neighbors near and far (Mark 12:31), and as a way to engage in justice work (Micah 6:8)—is an effective

reframe whenever I think about the vocational purpose behind my public-facing work.[25]

Key Takeaways

1. Intentional sampling is needed for addressing the issue of representation in psychological research. At the same time, when targeting cultural groups, researchers must clearly articulate justification for it.
2. Distrust of researchers, power differences between researchers and participants, and misuse of research findings (e.g., strengthening of a cultural stereotype) can add to the difficulty in recruiting diverse research participants.
3. Comparison studies can intentionally or unintentionally perpetuate a message that one group is superior to the other.
4. Addressing intrapersonal motivation for conducting cultural research is important. In particular, *humility* as a posture can serve as an antidote to many of the misguided motivations in cultural research.
5. Public dissemination of research findings can be reframed as an intentional act of service to others.

Activities and Discussion Questions

1. Answer the following only if you have experience designing and implementing your own research study in psychology:
   a. Reflect on your motivation for doing the study. Did the deficit perspective and the desire to be a "savior" play a role? Looking back, what were some cultural stereotypes

25. P. Kim, "Tale of Two 'Tapes.'"

that might have biased your conceptualization or interpretation of findings?

   b. Were you able to give back to the community after your study concluded? In what ways? Was this done in a joyous spirit with a genuine posture of service, or was it done more transactionally?

2. Find a research article in psychology with (1) a clear Christian theme (e.g., an examination of an empirical relationship between a faith-based variable and a psychological outcome) and (2) an intentional focus on culture (e.g., a non-White sample). Some of the journals you might consider browsing are *Journal of Psychology and Theology*, *Journal of Psychology and Christianity*, *Christian Higher Education*, and *International Journal of Christianity and Education*.
   a. Is the justification for cultural focus clearly articulated?
   b. Is there a comparative methodology that intentionally or unintentionally signals a deficit?
   c. Did the authors demonstrate humility in their approach to answering their research questions? In their sampling?
   d. If you were to do the study over again, what might you change in light of the ideas presented in this chapter?

Case Study

Ronald is a psychology major. His advanced research method course requires a group research project to be conceptualized and implemented as an online survey. After some initial discussions, his group is entertaining the idea of examining psychological well-being and its relation to religiosity in a sample of Ethiopian college students. Ronald's group is optimistic that they can recruit a decent-sized sample of Ethiopian college students on their campus to participate in an online survey. This research question was inspired when one of the group members attended a chapel service that featured an Ethiopian guest speaker. Ronald's group is made up of two women and three men; all group members identify as White American. One of the group members, Clara, has a roommate who is the president of the Black Student Union (BSU) on campus; she is positive that BSU has members who are of Ethiopian heritage.

Imagine that you are a student in Ronald's group and reflect on these questions:

1. What might you propose as the next step(s) in the group project?
2. What are some of the ethical concerns that might arise as you progress in conceptualizing and implementing this research study?
3. What Christian values might underlie what you decide to do?
4. Would you consider a comparison study? Why or why not?

3

The Said Versus the Unsaid

Cross-Cultural Communication

Growing up, I dreaded going out to eat at restaurants with other families—but not because I did not enjoy the opportunity to eat out. Rather, I knew what was likely coming at the conclusion of the meal: a demonstrative "argument" between my parents and their friends to decide who would pay. Sometimes the interaction would turn somewhat physical, such as one person holding the arm of another person to prevent them from paying. And then, just as quickly as things escalated, one person would end up paying, and the others acquiesced.

Throughout this ordeal, I would sink deeper into my chair, embarrassed beyond measure by this interaction between the adults.

Only later in my life did I learn that fighting for the bill was a cultural dance of sorts involving sophisticated forms of communication. All along, everyone involved knew who would end up paying the bill. But the cultural value of preserving and saving face meant that there needed to be a certain type of interaction—communication—before the person who was supposed to pay actually paid.

How Important Is Context?

When psychologists engage in the topic of communication across cultures, they often turn to differences that might exist due to context (i.e., what is unsaid) versus words (i.e., what is said). In the above vignette, what is uttered as verbal communication ("I will pay!") is not as relevant as the behaviors of the folks who are involved. Furthermore, what has a pivotal role in communication is the background—history, one might say—regarding who paid last time the families dined out together. Additionally, it might also be important to keep in mind who is in a position of power (e.g., older, more financially achieved). Together, these unspoken aspects might outweigh the importance of spoken words.

Introducing the varying degrees of value that cultures place on *context* in communication, anthropologist Edward T. Hall writes that culture serves to "provide a highly selective screen between man and the outside world."[1] According to this image, culture functions as a filter that allows interpersonal communication to occur according to the norms put forward in a given context. Hall goes on to bifurcate communication as either dependent on context (high-context communication) or independent of it (low-context communication).[2] High-context communication is a style of sending messages interpersonally using contextual factors, such as nonverbals and shared history. In low-context communication, what comes out of the mouth or is written down is regarded as the more ideal form of interpersonal communication. It might be described as explicit communication.

Beyond the descriptions of high- and low-context communication styles, it is also helpful to understand the advantages and challenges associated with these styles. Let's start with high-context communication. One advantage of high-context communication is the ability to maintain social harmony and preserve social face.[3]

1. Hall, *Beyond Culture*, 85.
2. Hall, *Beyond Culture*, 91.
3. Mio et al., *Multicultural Psychology*, 144–45.

That is, one might be motivated to engage in high-context communication when the primary goal in the interaction is to maintain social harmony and not embarrass oneself or others. Going back to the opening story about families "fighting" to pay the bill at a restaurant, this type of cultural dance can help the party that ultimately does not pay preserve their social dignity because at least they gave it their best attempt. And the party who does end up paying is also socially honored because, well, they actually paid. Therefore, a main advantage of high-context communication is that it is something that preserves and even deepens existing relationships.

One might surmise, then, that a potential pitfall of low-context communication is that, at times, it can put the needs of the individual over the needs of the others, increasing the risk of fracturing relationships or disturbing social harmony. Furthermore, low-context communication can come across as brash, rude, and not considerate of the feelings of the recipient. As an example, Sanne Schinkel and coauthors studied the perspectives of Turkish-Dutch participants in the Netherlands about engaging with medical doctors. One of the key findings was the participants' wish that their doctors would employ more high-context communication with them; the participants felt their doctors' preference for more low-context communication served as a barrier for clear engagement.[4]

Another advantage of high-context communication is that it allows for shortcuts to be taken when communicating with others.[5] That is, shared knowledge or experience can lead to individuals being able to jump right in to a particular exchange. Returning to the opening example again, the individuals involved could engage in their back-and-forth because they had a shared history, such as doing this exchange in the past. Contrast that with a scenario in which someone who does not know about this ritual is thrust into it; the communication will not go well at all because that person

4. Schinkel et al., "Perceptions of Barriers," 1473.
5. Hall, *Beyond Culture*, 101.

lacks the background information and experience to make the interaction work.

Therefore, one drawback of high-context communication is the potential for miscommunication. That is, the felt or understood message on the part of the recipient might differ, sometimes radically so, from the intended message. As an example, a focus group study analyzed the responses of Nairobi youths to sexual abstinence posters. The authors of this study reported that both high- and low-context communication played important roles in the messaging. In particular, participants reported confusion around some of the details of the fliers; the authors noted that although the explicit messaging of the campaign might have been clear, the contextual messaging was problematic and served as a barrier to clear delivery. One example was the socioeconomic differences among the youth participants, such that youths from lower socioeconomic statuses perceived discrepant messaging behind the unspoken aspects of the campaign compared to those in a higher socioeconomic status.[6]

Another potential "disadvantage" (in quotes because the longer and more arduous path might not necessarily be a disadvantage) of high-context communication is that it requires intentional time to be invested prior to the actual transmission of a message.[7] And in situations that require messages to be conveyed quickly sans the consideration for contextual factors such as relationship history, with significant consequences if they are not (e.g., yelling "Stop!" to a child about to run into the path of a car), high-context communication can feel quite counterproductive. In the opening vignette, the interaction is longer in duration than what might have happened if, consistent with my younger self's desperate wish, the folks involved just verbally communicated about who might pay. In that sense, there are situations when less time and energy are exerted with explicit verbal communication. For example,

6. Muraya et al., "Implications of High-/Low-Context Communication," 519–22.
7. Hall, *Beyond Culture*, 101.

in Japan, slow response, or the lack of response altogether, following a crisis can be partly explained by cultural preference for high-context communication.[8] Relatedly, sometimes the hierarchical emphasis of a culture can make the conversation much more roundabout to preserve the face of those in positions of power. In relationships such as the one between a clinical supervisee and supervisor, where constructive and candid feedback is required for professional growth, high-context communication norms might prevent those of lower status from effectively communicating with their supervisors.[9]

Pause to Reflect

Reflect on your own preferences for communicating with another person. Do you prefer communication to be straightforward, where the person says what they mean? Or do you prioritize the protection of feelings and relational harmony, even if the verbal aspect of communication might be compromised as a result? Perhaps you value both? What are some cultural influences on your preferences?

Correlates of Preference for High- and Low-Context Communication

Who might prefer each type of communication style? Some scholars have approached this question using a national-level analysis. One such approach assessed the preference for direct communication and reported on the differences among individuals representing several different countries. This approach and resulting evidence can be somewhat helpful in making some broad brushstrokes about national characteristics. For example, US participants scored higher on a measure of direct communication than participants

8. Cooper-Chen and Tanaka, "Public Relations in Japan," 103–4.
9. Bang and Goodyear, "South Korean Supervisees' Experience," 370.

from Japan.[10] At the same time, this method's shortcoming is that it could lead to generalizations about communication preferences that are not rooted in a more nuanced understanding of culture.

Therefore, an alternative is to examine how various cultural constructs that a person has internalized might be associated with or predictive of communication-style preferences. In this way, more definitive conclusions can be drawn as to possible cultural explanations for why one might more readily turn to various communication methods. In a sample of Asian Americans, traditional Asian cultural values, such as emotional restraint, were associated with more frequent reliance on indirect communication.[11] More commonly, scholars have asserted that collectivistic tendencies and closely related constructs tend to be associated with reliance on high-context communication. Self-construal, or how one defines oneself, was also found to be related to communication-style preference.[12] For instance, an independent self-construal is predictive of less reliance on indirect messages, whereas an interdependent self-construal is associated with more sensitivity to others' feelings.[13] Consistent with this finding, a study compared McDonald's advertising content across cultures and reported that the ad content in high-context cultures had a certain distinctiveness compared to low-context cultures. For example, high-context cultures tended to have more themes that featured relational or communal aspects than low-context cultures.[14] In sum, high- and low-context communication-style preferences are intricately related to various cultural norms and values.

A Biblical Perspective on Communication Styles

Christian communities understand the importance of clear, effective, and edifying communication with one another. The Bible

10. H. Park et al., "Individual and Cultural Variations," 182.
11. Y. Park and Kim, "Asian and European American Cultural Values," 51–53.
12. Markus and Kitayama, "Culture and the Self," 226–29.
13. Gudykunst et al., "Influence of Cultural Individualism-Collectivism," 536.
14. Würtz, "Intercultural Communication," 283–98.

is filled with stories and exhortations toward competent communication; it also contains warnings against inadequate communication. In particular, Proverbs is full of wisdom about what constitutes healthy communication versus unhealthy communication: "A gentle answer turns away wrath, but a harsh word stirs up anger" (15:1); "the words of the reckless pierce like swords, but the tongue of the wise brings healing" (12:18); "the soothing tongue is a tree of life, but a perverse tongue crushes the spirit" (15:4). It is clear that there is wisdom in perceiving the act of communication, regardless of whether it is high-context or low-context, as something that can inflict emotional wounds or be incredibly life-giving. Both high-context and low-context styles of communication have the capability to do both.

Moreover, I am struck by the life of Jesus and how he engaged in effective communication that could be characterized as high-context or indirect. The well-known story of Lazarus includes moments of high-context communication that at initial glance could be characterized as puzzling or ineffective. Somewhat cryptically, but also correctly in retrospect, Jesus tells the disciples, "Lazarus has fallen asleep; but I am going there to wake him up" (John 11:11). The disciples understandably think Jesus is saying that Lazarus is sleeping, when in fact Jesus is saying that Lazarus has died. Later in the story, Jesus responds to the grief of his loved ones, such as Mary, by demonstrating radical empathy: Jesus weeps (11:35). A staunch proponent of low-context communication might argue that this nonverbal communication of empathy is not needed and that a direct or low-context communication of "Do not worry; I am going to raise Lazarus from the dead in a bit" would have been a better alternative. From an efficiency perspective, the latter would have been a superior response, one that would have saved much time and emotional energy.

But instead, Jesus demonstrates ultimate humanity by nonverbally mirroring the grief of those whom he deeply loves. Even though he knows the factual outcome—Lazarus will be brought to life eventually—his priority is not swift and accurate deliverance of the message. Instead, Jesus clearly elevates the meaningful connection that occurs through the high-context communication of weeping.

And it is not like Jesus lacks the skills or the propensity to be direct in communication. This is apparent even in the Lazarus story. When Jesus is about to raise Lazarus from the dead, he gives super clear instructions—low-context—both to those around him ("Take away the stone," John 11:39) and to Lazarus when instructing him to come out of the tomb. There is no mistaking the concreteness and clarity of this type of communication from Jesus. There are other examples of low-context communication as well. When he tells the merchants at the temple, "Stop turning my Father's house into a market!" (John 2:16), he is quite literal. Or when Jesus tells his disciples to give food to the five thousand gathered and hungry (see Matt. 14:13–21), his disciples might have wished he used high-context communication in his instructions.

Of Nunchi, Power, and Jesus

Cultures have norms around interpersonal communication that are internalized by their members. At the same time, some cultural constructs, for various reasons, can transcend national borders and garner global interest. Euny Hong, writing for a non-Korean audience in her book *The Power of Nunchi: The Korean Secret to Happiness and Success*, argues that her readers might do well to understand and implement the skill of *nunchi* in their everyday lives. Hong defines *nunchi* as "the subtle art of gauging other people's thoughts and feelings to build harmony, trust, and connection."[15] Does this sound familiar? That's right—nunchi is a prime example of a cultural norm that emphasizes high-context communication. Going deeper, the cultural construct of nunchi is a critical skill that all Koreans are expected to acquire. Nunchi reflects the interpersonal skill of understanding social cues

15. E. Hong, *Power of Nunchi*, 1.

and nonverbals and acting on them as called for. It is the ability to accurately and promptly size up a room. Fittingly, in the Korean language a deficit in nunchi is described as such—"that person lacks nunchi"—with the implication being that a person is expected to have a baseline level of nunchi. But someone who displays exceptional nunchi is described as having "fast" nunchi, implying that superior interpersonal communication requires the ability to take prompt and decisive action.

Going even deeper, although nunchi can manifest in all types of interpersonal communications, a hierarchical society like South Korea especially emphasizes it as a way for someone in a position of power or authority to be served by others.[16] That is, someone of lower status is expected to have fast nunchi so that those above them (e.g., a supervisor, elderly members of the family, customers) can have their various needs met. Does your boss need something done? Someone with fast nunchi will get it done, even in the absence of verbal communication. Do you suspect that your elderly uncle needs another glass of wine at the family dinner? You will be praised for having quick nunchi if you pour him another glass. Do you sense that your professor is rushed to get the classroom set up before class, so one day you decide to get materials set up in the classroom before the professor arrives? Again, that is rapid nunchi. And you get the point: Nunchi is often the ingredient that allows someone—typically in a position of power, status, or influence—to be served by others.

But what if this interpersonal dynamic underlying nunchi (and by extension, high-context communication) gets flipped? That is, what if nunchi is used by those of higher status to serve those who have less power? Those with fewer resources?

Jesus said that he "did not come to be served, but to serve, and to give his life as a ransom for many" (Matt. 20:28). And he truly lived out this life of servanthood during his time on this earth. I

16. For more on nunchi and power dynamics, including additional biblical examples, see P. Kim, "Korean Constructs"; also see P. Kim, "Redeeming Korean Constructs," 27:46.

would argue that he demonstrated *radical* nunchi for the pains and sufferings of all those who interacted with him. That is, nunchi was a way for him to pay careful attention to the nonverbals surrounding him, allowing him to act in compassion. The Bible is full of so many examples, but here are a few:

In John 4, Jesus quickly recognizes the true struggles of the Samaritan woman at the well—that underlying the conversation about water is a deeper longing to be seen and accepted. He senses this need without any words being uttered, and he acts on it.

There is the time that Jesus washes the feet of the disciples in John 13. In this passage, it is striking that right before washing the disciples' feet Jesus realizes that Judas has already been prompted to betray him (v. 2) and that "the Father had put all things under his [Jesus's] power, and that he had come from God and was returning to God" (v. 3). What follows is not a verbal communication about these profound realizations but instead the act of washing the disciples' feet. This famous act of servanthood and humility is one that radically flipped the relationship dynamic between the leader and those who follow. In the context of nunchi, it could be argued that the situation goes counter to how nunchi typically operates—the leader (Jesus), not those who are serving him, is first to act.

And then there is the story of the woman who has been bleeding for twelve years and feels so desperate for healing that she decides to touch the corner of Jesus's outfit. No words are uttered—just a quick touch. Jesus, though, knows what this nonverbal means, and again, he acts on it to miraculously heal this woman (Luke 8:43–48).

Mark 6:34 reads, "When Jesus landed and saw a large crowd, he had compassion on them, because they were like sheep without a shepherd. So he began teaching them many things." I would assert that this verse is a fitting example of nunchi as well: being able to feel the room (or the crowd, in this case), ultimately feel compassion, and take appropriate action (i.e., teaching them) on the basis of the assessment. Amazingly, it is the Almighty God who demonstrates rapid nunchi to the longings of our hearts and minds. And this loving God takes swift action to intervene, even without explicit verbal communication from us.

Likewise, those of us who claim to be followers of Jesus should strive to live like Jesus in this regard. We should be extra-attuned to the pains and sufferings of those around us. At times distress is communicated using words; other times, we must pick up on high-context communication. As Christians, may we be diligent in our commitment to pay attention to both the spoken and the unspoken needs of others. As Robert Pierce, founder of World Vision, is known to have prayed, "Let my heart be broken with the things that break the heart of God."[17]

Key Takeaways

1. High-context communication is when individuals rely on nonverbals and contextual information for delivery of messages.
2. Low-context communication is when people primarily use verbals (i.e., spoken or written words) for conveying messages interpersonally.
3. Both communication-style preferences are motivated by certain goals, and they both have advantages and disadvantages.
4. Research demonstrates that communication-style preferences tend to be associated with cultural constructs (e.g., interdependent understanding of self is correlated with high-context communication).
5. Scriptures provide exhortations toward and warnings against different styles of communication. Jesus's life includes notable examples of high- and low-context communications.

17. Stearns, "Blessed by a Broken Heart."

6. The Korean cultural construct of nunchi is a prime example of a cultural emphasis on high-context communication. In particular, it typically describes a person in lower social status (e.g., a subordinate in a job setting) having the ability to quickly pick up on the needs of those in higher status (e.g., a boss) and act on such information.
7. Jesus's life includes exemplary moments when he flips the interpersonal dynamics of nunchi by serving others; this is something that Christians should emulate so that they can serve others who are in need.

Activities and Discussion Questions

1. Find other biblical references about interpersonal communication in the Scriptures. Code each one as high- or low-context or both.
2. Can you think of examples from your own life where low-context communication was effective? Ineffective? How about high-context communication? What made these communication styles effective or ineffective?
3. Who or what was most influential in shaping your interpersonal communication tendencies? Especially reflect on cultural influences.

Case Study

Jessa Mae is an international student from the Philippines studying at a Christian university in the US. Lately she has been experiencing some frustrations with her American roommate about cleaning and organizing the room. In particular, Jessa Mae would like her roommate to be more proactive in keeping the room clean and organized. Jessa Mae has tried many things to communicate her frustration to her roommate, such as giving subtle hints about cleaning (e.g., purposefully organizing the room when her roommate is around), but nothing has worked. What started out as an annoyance has now blossomed into a major source of stress for Jessa Mae. She finally approached her residence adviser (RA), who was sympathetic toward her frustrations. After listening to her, the RA advised her to "be direct in communication" with her roommate. Jessa Mae pushed back, saying, "But that's not my style; I am not sure how to do that." The RA responded, "Well, the Bible says that we are to speak truth to one another in love. If you are unwilling to do that, then you are not living out your Christian life in a way pleasing to God."

1. If you were the RA in this situation, how might you respond to Jessa Mae, keeping in mind what you know about intercultural communication? How might the roommate also be pulled into the conversation?
2. How might organizations, such as universities, structure their outreach programming so that diverse communication styles are honored? What might this type of posture look like in a cultural context like the US, which tends to place a higher premium on low-context communication?

4

More Precision Needed

Collectivism and Individualism

The kingdom of God is big enough for both collectivists and individualists to live together.

—Euiwan Cho, "Kingdom of God"

In my years of teaching cross-cultural psychology to American college students, collectivism has been the cultural construct most frequently raised by students during classroom conversations. It is also one of the more misunderstood constructs. It seems like whenever students encounter a cultural practice that deviates from what is typical in the US (e.g., co-sleeping), they often point to collectivism as an explanation for the cross-cultural difference. Although there might be occasions when using collectivism to describe a behavior is legitimate—for instance, collectivism has been empirically identified as one of the cultural values prevalent among Asian Americans[1]—too many times collectivism (and its

1. B. Kim et al., "Asian American Values Scale," 191.

partner, individualism) can end up causing the oversimplification of complex and nuanced realities of culture. This type of over-reliance on collectivism is widespread in psychology as well. In response, scholars have called for more precision when researching and teaching about these constructs, going beyond the simplistic and diffused framework of the collectivism-individualism dichotomy.[2] As a remedy, scholars have called for alternative and specific constructs to be examined in lieu of the broader collectivism and individualism framework.[3] In response to this call, this chapter is for those interested in further exploring this topic from a Christian perspective.

I will first define four constructs in light of the work of Triandis and Gelfand: vertical collectivism, horizontal collectivism, vertical individualism, and horizontal individualism.[4] I then will share some cross-cultural illustrations of these four constructs, mainly drawing from the world of sports. Finally, I will provide some Christian perspectives regarding the four constructs.

Pause to Reflect

First, do a quick self-reflection based on what is true for you when it comes to the different types of collectivism and individualism. Read the below descriptions of each type and see what might be true for you.[a]

- In your worldview, do you emphasize the distinctiveness of the individual from others? If so, you might highly endorse horizontal individualism.
- In your worldview, do you believe that competition, or outdoing another person, is important in life? If so, you might be emphasizing vertical individualism.

2. Wong et al., "Emperor with No Clothes," 257–58; P. Kim, "Resisting the Allure."

3. Wong et al., "Emperor with No Clothes," 257–58.

4. Triandis and Gelfand, "Converging Measurement."

- Do you value interconnectedness with the people around you, such as your peers or communities? If so, you likely have a strong sense of horizontal collectivism.
- Finally, do you emphasize social hierarchy or respect for authority figures in your relationships? If so, you likely have a strong sense of vertical collectivism.

Which type of individualism or collectivism do you most strongly identify with? Do you have examples from your life for each of the four types?

[a]These descriptions of the four constructs are summarized from Triandis and Gelfand, "Converging Measurement," 118–19.

Key Terms and Examples from Cross-Cultural Contexts

Horizontal individualism focuses on the distinctiveness of the individual.[5] It is the dimension of individualism that is arguably the most popular; the uniqueness of a person is often equated with the notion that someone or a community might value individualism. In a seminal article, Markus and Kitayama describe an independent view of the person as a framework that attempts to clearly differentiate—draw appropriate boundaries—between the self and relationships that make up the interpersonal network.[6]

Gannon and Pillai write that American football is an example of a team sport that, ironically, has strong horizontally individualistic aspects.[7] The authors argue that another way to think about individualism is to capture the level of specialized roles that people in a community might have; in essence, specialization is a way of drawing clear boundaries between what I do and what the person next to me does so that our roles do not overlap. Gannon and Pillai

5. Triandis and Gelfand, "Converging Measurement," 119.
6. Markus and Kitayama, "Culture and the Self," 226.
7. Gannon and Pillai, *Understanding Global Cultures*, 248–72.

give the example of someone whose job is to carry the American football coach's communication gear to prevent the coach from tripping. Similarly, and fascinatingly, some football teams hire a "get-back coach" to pull the hyperfocused and sometimes (often?) angry head coach back to the proper place on the sideline so that the team can avoid being penalized by the referee; the get-back coach's specialized and unique role is to grab the coach by the waist and literally pull them back multiple times during the game.[8] In observing how prominent American cultural values are illustrated through American football, Gannon and Pillai write that these values "reflect a high degree of specialized individualism that expresses itself within the structure of a team."[9]

Vertical individualism is also a type of individualism but is characterized by a mentality of outdoing the other person (read: hierarchy).[10] It is a cultural value characterized by a competitive spirit. It is about doing better, looking better, feeling better, and so on. Even if you are a casual follower of sports, you will realize that it is rather easy to identify vertical individualism as a driving force behind most sporting events. Not everyone gets a trophy in serious competition, and the winners are those who outdo the other individuals in the competition. I love watching swimming (or any other racing events) because it is one of those sports in which you can, in real time, observe the hierarchy develop. In swimming competition broadcasts, the overhead camera angle captures this hierarchy so clearly: a few in the front, a couple more in the middle of the pack, and a few, who clearly do not have a chance of winning but are competing hard, in the rear.

In professional baseball, Barry Bonds broke—really, *smashed*—the all-time home run record in Major League Baseball (MLB), but it was found later that he took banned steroids to achieve it. By many accounts, Bonds was motivated to do this because he felt envious of the other players who had broken the home run record

8. Moriarty, "Sean McVay Has a Get-Back Coach."
9. Gannon and Pillai, *Understanding Global Cultures*, 257.
10. Triandis and Gelfand, "Converging Measurement," 119.

in recent years, and he wanted to surpass their accomplishments.[11] That is a classic example of vertical individualism.

Let me deviate from sports for a moment. Political actions can also be driven by vertical individualism. President Donald Trump posted the following message on Twitter (now X) after a threatening message from the North Korean leader Kim Jong Un: "North Korean Leader Kim Jong Un just stated that the 'Nuclear Button is on his desk at all times.' Will someone from his depleted and food starved regime please inform him that I too have a Nuclear Button, but it is a much bigger & more powerful one than his, and my Button works!"[12] "Bigger and more powerful" is a sentiment that drives vertical individualism.

Returning to baseball, one of my favorite leisure activities when spending time in South Korea is to attend a professional baseball game. The rules of the sport itself are pretty much the same around the world, but the behaviors of the people—both fans and players—often illustrate some of the key differences between collectivism and individualism. The emphasis on both hierarchical connectedness (vertical collectivism) and interconnectedness with others (horizontal collectivism)[13] is apparent whenever I attend baseball games in Korea, in contrast to the MLB games that I have attended in the US.

For example, in the MLB, whenever a player reaches first base, it is common for him to interact with the first baseman by doing things like striking up a casual conversation or exchanging friendly daps. In South Korea this interaction between the first baseman and base runner often comes with a fascinating culture-specific variation: The younger player in the interaction will remove his hat and quickly bow to the older player, and the older player will likely respond with a pat on the backside or some other way of acknowledging the greeting (e.g., a nodding of the head). You will also see

11. Curry, "Jealousy Led Bonds."

12. Donald J. Trump (@realDonaldTrump), Twitter (now X), January 2, 2018, https://twitter.com/realDonaldTrump/status/948355557022420992?s=20.

13. Triandis and Gelfand, "Converging Measurement," 119.

a similar interaction if a batter is accidentally hit by a pitch from a younger pitcher; the pitcher will apologize with a deeper bow. Usually, the batter will accept the apology and indicate that he is fine by nodding or raising a hand reassuringly. These brief but unmistakable interactions are examples of vertical collectivism: respect for social hierarchy and, in this case, a hierarchy that is based on age. Even in a competitive sporting event that is meant to even out the playing field, vertical collectivism clearly manifests in this way.

Then there is horizontal collectivism, which prizes connectedness to one another.[14] Of course, both MLB and Korean Baseball Organization (KBO) fans share in cheering loudly for their teams. But there are several aspects of cheering in the KBO that illustrate horizontal collectivism. First, KBO cheering is done in complete unison, with thousands of people joining in. In the MLB a typical baseball game will include several different types of noises, such as unintelligible yelling from those who have had one too many drinks, folks shouting words of appreciation or insult to the players, music on full blast that sometimes drowns out all other sounds, and the roar of the crowd, which includes many different noises forming a single sound. In contrast, South Korean baseball fans cheer in perfect synchrony. Each home team batter who comes to the plate is assigned a unique song, complete with a full set of lyrics, and everyone sings their heart out. Moreover, all songs and cheers are accompanied by a full dance routine choreographed and led by a group of professional cheerleaders.

Esal was a psychology student at my US institution. As part of her study-abroad experience in South Korea, she attended a Korean baseball game. Here is a recollection of the event in her own words, especially as it connects to themes like unity and social harmony:

> Aside from a high school football game, I have never attended a sports event, so I was not very excited about going to the baseball

14. Triandis and Gelfand, "Converging Measurement," 119.

> game. I grew up watching cricket and football with my parents and never understood their excitement for the games. The games are slow to follow, and the crowd usually looked dead. I was expecting the same energy at the Korean baseball game, but to my surprise, there was hardly a dull moment. When we came in, we were given a paper banner to hold up during chants, like what fans receive at K-pop concerts. In front of our seats, there was a stage for the cheerleaders. They began by dancing to a few popular songs to get the crowd riled up and excited. Then, as each player entered the field, the cheerleaders guided the audience to recite a chant along with the assigned hand gestures. I was shocked at how synchronized the audience was, and I was jealous that Koreans get to see an entertaining performance at every baseball game. Americans have solely reserved that engagement and excitement for the Super Bowl ads and halftime show. Toward the end, I had completely lost track of who was winning, but I was determined to get the chants right and blend in with the crowd despite not knowing what I was saying.[15]

Another aspect of horizontal collectivism is that you are connected with not just anyone but particularly to others who share in your own identity. That is, the in-group versus out-group mentality is especially strong in an interdependent context.[16] In the MLB, it is not uncommon to see fans of the away team scattered here and there among the home crowd. They sometimes receive friendly banter from the home fans, and occasionally the interactions turn combative. But it is an accepted reality that these away fans proudly donning the "enemy" jerseys will coexist among the majority who are rooting for the home team. The away fans also show up at KBO games. But in contrast to their American counterparts, they sit together in a designated section, typically behind the third base line; the seats are unmistakable, brightly colored and accompanied by their own cheerleading platform.

15. Esal Shakil, online communication to author, January 17, 2024.
16. See Markus and Kitayama, "Culture and the Self," 229.

As a result, the in-group and out-group membership is clearly differentiated at a KBO game.

Christian Perspectives

In psychological science, an interdependent understanding of the person is best conceptualized as *orthogonal* to an independent conceptualization. That is, interdependence and independence (or collectivism and individualism) are not necessarily dependent on each other, and therefore both dimensions should be considered for a more complete understanding of the self.[17] As a simple example, it is possible for a person to strongly endorse both the interdependent and the independent understanding of the self. I am struck by this notion's compatibility with how Christian traditions and Scriptures perceive the role of collectivism and individualism. As the opening quote of this chapter states, an important recognition is that a redeemed understanding of these constructs should not leave us compartmentalizing the two ways of being and relating; instead, we must find a way to keep in mind the larger body while recognizing the distinctiveness of the individual. That is, from a Christian perspective, we are called to embrace parts of collectivism and individualism, but we are also warned about the potential perils of these ways of relating to one another. Note that commentaries on collectivism and individualism in a Christian perspective have tended to focus on a broader conceptualization of these belief systems, essentially treating them as horizontal collectivism and horizontal individualism.[18] Below, in addition to perspectives on the horizontal dimensions, I also provide perspectives on the vertical aspects of collectivism and individualism.

17. Singelis, "Measurement of Independent and Interdependent Self-Construals," 581–87.

18. E.g., see Cho, "Kingdom of God."

Vertical Collectivism

Let's start with vertical collectivism. Several biblical exhortations underscore the importance of vertical collectivism for faithful Christians. Jesus himself speaks about the value of honoring social hierarchy when he instructs his followers to "give back to Caesar what is Caesar's" (Mark 12:17). Moreover, throughout the Bible, parents are especially highlighted as deserving of respect and honor. Honoring parents is described as a virtue that will lead to longevity and prosperity for the child (Exod. 20:12; Eph. 6:2–3). Similarly, the book of Proverbs is full of instructions expressing sentiments like "Listen to your father, who gave you life, and do not despise your mother when she is old" (23:22). The book of Proverbs also makes it abundantly clear that elderly persons are to be respected for their wisdom and experience, stating, "Gray hair is a crown of splendor; it is attained in the way of righteousness" (16:31). Likewise, Job 12:12 asks, "Is not wisdom found among the aged? Does not long life bring understanding?" Finally, honoring folks who are older also includes caring for the elderly: "Do not rebuke an older man harshly, but exhort him as if he were your father. Treat younger men as brothers, older women as mothers, and younger women as sisters, with absolute purity" (1 Tim. 5:1–2). In sum, the pursuit of faithful Christian living includes the understanding that part of God's design and order for humanity is for people to honor those who are older, wiser, more experienced, and so on.

Of course, the Bible also *cautions* against vertical collectivism applied in a distorted way. Several well-known biblical figures fell from their positions of authority and power at least partly, one can surmise, because they were blinded by their own statuses. King Solomon comes to mind as a ready example of someone who enjoyed some amazing riches and power but ultimately ended up described as someone who "did evil in the eyes of the LORD" (1 Kings 11:6). The Bible also warns about the potential dangers of abusing the authority of some positions of power. For example, teachers are given these cautionary words: "Not many of you should become teachers, my fellow believers, because you know that we who teach will be judged more strictly" (James 3:1). And then there are the exhortations for those who are older, including parents, to be careful about their elevated status. For instance, parents are cautioned, "Fathers, do not exasperate your children; instead, bring them up in the training and instruction of the Lord" (Eph. 6:4). Here is another one: "Fathers, do not embitter your children, or they will become discouraged" (Col. 3:21). In both examples there is a call to understand that vertical collectivism could go awry, resulting in anger but also a sense of discouragement for the one who has less power (i.e., the child).

Christianity Today's critically acclaimed podcast series *The Rise and Fall of Mars Hill* chronicles the success and eventual downfall of the megachurch Mars Hill under the leadership of its charismatic leader, Mark Driscoll. While not placing the entirety of the blame on Driscoll, the podcast does emphasize how vertical collectivism gone astray can lead to a community's downfall.[19] Put differently, the sinful side of vertical collectivism can rear its ugly head as spiritual abuse, narcissism, and lack of accountability. The story of Mars Hill is a good reminder to the Christian community that vertical collectivism as a value and posture needs to be partnered with a structure of accountability.

Horizontal Collectivism

There are ample favorable references in the Bible about living out horizontal collectivism. For example, we are called to be involved in one another's lives, as we are part of one body (1 Cor. 12:12–27). We see examples of early Christians being in fellowship with one another (Acts 2:42). The fellowship we are called to with believers

19. Mike Cosper, host, *The Rise and Fall of Mars Hill*, podcast, produced by Erik Petrik, *Christianity Today*, 2021–22, https://www.christianitytoday.com/podcasts/the-rise-and-fall-of-mars-hill.

looks different from the fellowship we have with nonbelievers (Gal. 6:10). We are also told to consider ourselves in a lower position than others (Phil. 2:3) and to demonstrate empathy for both positive and negative emotions that others are experiencing (e.g., Rom. 12:15). Taken together, these are examples of how being a part of one body in Christ is foundational to Christian living.

How can horizontal collectivism pose a deviation from what God wills for us? As in that KBO baseball stadium, where the demarcation between friends and foes (or my team and your team) is abundantly clear, Christian communities can also easily fall into the trap of the us-versus-them mentality, which in turn can contribute to an unhealthily insular community. Don't get me wrong; there is something valuable and necessary about connecting with fellow believers. But when we overvalue the comfort of being with one another, it can lead to a lack of engagement with those who are outside the Christian faith. Put differently, we fail to love our neighbors—the biblical mandate does not qualify that those neighbors whom we love must be Christian (Mark 12:31). In sum, when it comes to the appeal of horizontal collectivism, we must be careful to avoid the mentality that encourages affiliation with those who share a Christian worldview and distance from those who do not.

As noted earlier, this preference for one's "own people" is clearly identified in psychological science whenever the concept of in-group bias is discussed. Social identity theory argues that we tend to gravitate toward relationships with people who are like us and that such a natural pull has its function in forming individual identities.[20] Horizontal collectivism as a posture and belief system renders us especially vulnerable to this type of social insularity. As Euiwan Cho puts it, "At its worst, collectivism tends to be exclusive and hostile to the outside group while demanding the solidarity of the in-group. . . . It is an in-group mentality that

20. Tajfel and Turner, "Integrative Theory of Intergroup Conflict," 40–41.

constantly stigmatizes, hates, and expels others who are different from them."[21]

In some ways, this in-group mentality is easy for us as human beings. That's the way things are in our world. That's the natural pull. But a Christian worldview says that we must recognize this gravitation toward the in-group and actively counter it by connecting with those who are out of our inner circles.

Pause to Reflect

What are your social circles like? How might you live into the gospel truth that calls us to an interdependence with one another, going beyond the "easiest" people to be in connection with?

Horizontal Individualism

Horizontal individualism has its place—for example, honoring a person as a being who is created in the image of God. Indeed, there is something special about the deep recognition of one person's uniqueness and distinctiveness. First Corinthians 12 articulates how God has bestowed unique gifts to all of us and recognizes that these distinctive aspects must be understood in relation to the larger body.

I think about when Jesus scolded his overzealous disciples, telling them, "Let the little children come to me" (Matt. 19:14). To be fair, the disciples who were trying to prevent the young ones from reaching Jesus were likely well intentioned, keeping in mind things like vertical collectivism ("Children should not disturb adult conversations") and horizontal collectivism ("A few children should not disrupt the larger group"). But Jesus's radical approach in this story is one of seeing the value of the smaller unit—in this case, the children. Jesus's approach says that the larger group's

21. Cho, "Kingdom of God."

needs should not necessarily supersede the needs of the smaller unit. This sure seems like Jesus is readily endorsing the parts of individualism that emphasize the inherent value and autonomy of people.

But the same passage (1 Cor. 12) makes it abundantly clear that though the distinctiveness of the individual is honored, we must understand individualism in relation to the larger body. Verse 12 says, "Just as a body, though one, has many parts, but all its many parts form one body, so it is with Christ." And again, verse 27: "Now you are the body of Christ, and each one of you is a part of it." And the implication of this unity through diversity is that we should live in a way that honors connectedness: "If one part suffers, every part suffers with it; if one part is honored, every part rejoices with it" (v. 26).

Vertical Individualism

What about vertical individualism specifically? It is easy to think about the warnings against unhealthy competition and the resulting negative emotions, whether through the account of Cain and Abel in Genesis 4 or of King Saul being overcome with jealousy of young David in 1 Samuel 18.

Philippians 2:3–4 states, "Do nothing out of selfish ambition or vain conceit. Rather, in humility value others above yourselves, not looking to your own interests but each of you to the interests of the others." What is striking about this passage is that it does not instruct believers to not value themselves. Instead, it recognizes that while valuing the self is important and an expected thing to do, we must prioritize other people in a way that goes against our natural tendencies. In a world that is consistently broadcasting variations of the message "Take care of yourself first," faithful Christian living requires a radical counternarrative of turning the other cheek, of not insisting on "eye for eye" (Matt. 5:38–40).

Key Takeaways

1. Collectivism and individualism are often used to paint cross-cultural differences with broad brushstrokes. It is important to understand and apply more specific types of collectivism and individualism.
2. Horizontal individualism emphasizes the distinctiveness of the person, whereas vertical individualism captures the competitive drive underlying the way of relating to others.
3. Horizonal collectivism depicts the interpersonal connectedness of the person, whereas vertical collectivism is more concerned with the importance of hierarchical relationships.
4. Awareness of the strengths and dangers of collectivism and individualism from a Christian perspective will help us understand how we can live out these constructs in our own lives and guard against the pitfalls of each approach.

Activities and Discussion Questions

1. Think about a time when you used the word "collectivism" to refer to a person or culture. Which aspect(s) of collectivism (vertical or horizontal) did you actually mean? Do you feel like you used the word correctly?
2. Scan your social media feed and find real examples of horizontal/vertical collectivism and horizontal/vertical individualism. Which examples are easier to find, and what might this say about the cultural perspectives that tend to dominate your social circles?
3. What are some other biblical stories that illustrate aspects of collectivism? Individualism?
4. How does faithful Christian living translate to aspects of collectivism in your life? Individualism?

Case Study

Akira is a nineteen-year-old Japanese American college student. Her church college group is currently planning a short-term mission trip to Tijuana, Mexico. Each person in the college group has been asked to pay for their own trip. Because money has been tight, Akira is increasingly concerned about being able to participate in this church activity. She confided in her group leader about this difficulty. In their conversation, Akira also shared that her father, who lives in Japan, is a pastor of a church there. When learning of this detail, the group leader excitedly said, "Oh, I have an idea. Why don't you ask your father's church for financial support? You can write a letter requesting it." Hesitantly, Akira replied, "I know why you are suggesting that. But I am not sure I want to do that. That's not how they typically do things in Japan." The group leader paused with a puzzled look on her face and then responded, "But why not? It seems *biblical* to ask for money to do God's work."

1. How might collectivistic and individualistic frameworks have contributed to this clash of worldviews?
2. How might the group leader have responded differently to Akira's struggles?

5

Exploring and Committing

Stage Models of Cultural Identity Development

> Who am I? Where do I belong? How did I come to be this way? How will I be different in the future?

Questions about identity are foundational in psychological science. Erik Erikson, for example, asserts that people develop psychologically by resolving various conflicts or crises that arise across their lifetimes; moreover, he notes that the identity crisis that characterizes the adolescent years is an especially salient crisis to be resolved.[1]

Building on Erikson's model, James Marcia articulates that identity development takes place across two dimensions. First, identity is characterized by a sense of *commitment*, or a strength of attachment to a particular identity. Second, identity includes an *exploration*; that is, identity can be deepened through "trying out" and being open to different aspects of a culture. Combining these two key aspects of identity, Marcia describes four possible

1. Erikson, *Childhood and Society*, 247–74.

identity outcomes: identity achievement (high commitment, high exploration), moratorium (low commitment, high exploration), foreclosure (high commitment, low exploration), and identity diffusion (low commitment, low exploration).[2]

Pause to Reflect

Have you ever sought after (i.e., explored) an identity? Have you ever firmly landed on (i.e., committed to) a specific identity? Is commitment or exploration more salient for you?

Psychologist Jean Phinney conducted in-depth interviews with adolescents of color about their ethnic identities. In this study, Phinney found that the participants' responses about identity could be reliably coded as diffusion (a lack of thinking about identity), foreclosure (settling on an identity quickly, often because of others' influence), moratorium (lots of exploration but no commitment), and achieved (a balance between exploration and commitment), which was conceptualized as the best outcome.[3] A key lesson from this study was that adolescents of color have experiences that include both exploration and commitment to their ethnic identities, consistent with James Marcia's theorizing.

Jean Phinney is also the creator of a widely used ethnic identity measure in multicultural psychology, the Multigroup Ethnic Identity Measure. The measure assesses the individual's search for a sense of identity and their sense of having achieved or committed to an identity.[4]

2. Marcia, "Identity in Adolescence," 159–62.
3. Phinney, "Stages of Ethnic Identity Development," 42–44.
4. Phinney, "Multigroup Ethnic Identity Measure," 172; Phinney and Ong, "Conceptualization and Measurement," 276.

Models of Identity Development

Psychologists are drawn to cultural identity development models. A model of identity development attempts to model, often under the assumption of a linear progression, the complicated real-life process that is the development of cultural identity or identities.

Some models of cultural identity development attempt to capture the development broadly or comprehensively, and some are applicable to only specific cultural identities. Below are some examples.

A Comprehensive Model: R/CID

The Racial and Cultural Identity Development Model (R/CID) posits five stages of cultural identity development that are applicable across different groups.[5] The first is the *conformity* stage, and it is characterized by a sense of admiration and appreciation for those in the dominant cultural group. The individual might harbor a sense of inferiority about their own cultural group. Next is the *dissonance* stage. Here the individual experiences a feeling of discomfort at the realization that how they have viewed the world, including their identity and the dominant cultural identity, might not be reality. This realization moment might literally be a single moment (e.g., an Asian person seeing their Black friend mistreated at a store), or it might be a series of events—an accumulation of experiences—that moves the individual into this stage. Stage 3 is *resistance and immersion*, and it features a "deep plunge" into their own cultural background with a strong desire to learn more about their cultural heritage. On the flip side, there might be a sense of disdain for the majority culture. Stage 4 is *introspection*. Introspection is somewhat of a continuation of the

5. D. Sue and Sue, "Racial/Cultural Identity Development," 366–77. Also, p. 366 provides the brief history of how this model was articulated: It began with conceptualization from Atkinson et al., *Counseling American Minorities*, and then with some revisions from D. Sue and Sue, *Counseling the Culturally Different*, in the 2nd and 3rd editions.

resistance and immersion stage, but the difference is that it involves less intense emotions directed to the major or dominant culture and less favoring of the in-group. The individual might even start to branch out toward other minoritized cultures. The last stage is *integrative awareness*. In this final stage, the ideal balance between appreciation of one's own culture and other cultures is present, and there is a realistic understanding of the strengths and deficits of cultures, including one's own.[6]

Notice some of the fundamental questions that the stages of the R/CID are addressing: (1) How does one feel about the self? (2) How does one feel about one's own culture? (3) How does one feel about other minoritized groups? (4) How does one feel about people in social positions with more power?[7] These are the questions that come up in other models of cultural identity too. Also note that the earlier themes related to affinity, exploration, and commitment to an identity are embedded in these stages. Finally, there is an overall progression from a lack of awareness and commitment to a deeper awareness and commitment.

Pause to Reflect

Do you feel like the R/CID adequately captures your lived experiences? Why or why not? What are the positives of a model like this? Potential pitfalls?

Culture-Specific Identity Development Models

Another approach to cultural identity development models is to conceptualize a model that is applicable only to a particular group, such as a racial or ethnic group. The advantage of such an approach is that group-specific dynamics can be addressed; it is too simplistic to portray all cultural identities as developing in the

6. For more on the stages of R/CID, see D. Sue and Sue, "Racial/Cultural Identity Development," 366–77.

7. D. Sue and Sue, "Racial/Cultural Identity Development," 367.

same linear process. In particular, for communities of color in the US, there are some well-known stage models of identity development, such as the Nigrescence model for Black American identity.[8]

In the US, White Americans are less likely, compared to their Asian, Black, and Hispanic counterparts, to report that their race or ethnicity is important for self-perception.[9] Similarly, a qualitative study of White adults from the Midwest identified the denial of one's racial identity as a key theme.[10] Racial or ethnic identity among White individuals is linked to important outcomes, such as allyship[11] and the understanding of systemic racism.[12] Given these trends, it is vital for White Americans to thoughtfully engage the topic of White racial identity development. In the space below, I devote considerable space to articulate the stages of a well-known developmental model of White racial identity, and I integrate Christian faith considerations into this overview.

During a job interview many years ago, I was asked to deliver a short guest lecture. The lecture took place in a predominantly White classroom. At one point during my talk, I asked the students to engage in (what I thought was) a straightforward exercise: "Turn to the person next to you and share about your cultural background." To my surprise, this request was met with an awkward silence. After I sweated a bit at the unexpected lack of compliance from the students—remember, this was a job interview—a student raised their hand and thankfully provided an explanation: They had trouble participating in this exercise due to their White background. Since that time, I have had more interactions with White students expressing similar sentiments (e.g., "I can't do this assignment because I don't have a culture"). That is, it is not

8. Cross, "Negro-to-Black Conversion Experience," 15–25; for more on the Nigrescence model and other culture-specific models of identity development, see Mio et al., *Multicultural Psychology*, 258–78.

9. Horowitz et al., *Race in America 2019*, 13.

10. Dottolo and Stewart, "'I Never Think About My Race,'" 106–13.

11. Yantis, "Role of White Identity," 3–10.

12. Dull et al., "Learning (Not) to Know," 1004–11.

uncommon for me to encounter White students who are unable to engage in meaningful conversations about their White identities.

I have also had conversations with White students about their White identities that took an unexpected turn. One time, while we were covering the topic of racial discrimination, a White student in class told of being mistreated by their non-White high school peers. A session that had been designed to highlight the experiences of students of color quickly morphed into consoling this White student. Now, to be clear, this student's experience was legitimate; it is a form of trauma to experience harassment and bullying of any kind. But the emotional outburst and resulting communal response demonstrated how easy it is for a member of a majority culture to take over conversations about minoritized experiences.

Because White identity development is complicated and often misunderstood, psychologists find it helpful to rely on stage models to capture its progression. Janet Helms's White Racial Identity Development Model (WRIDM) is arguably the most famous of such models.[13]

Helms contends that for a White individual, a healthy sense of White racial development must involve wrestling with difficult questions around the topic of race. Like the cultural identity models described earlier, WRIDM begins with a status characterized by a lack of awareness (*contact*).[14] Someone in this status espouses a color-blind understanding of race and associated experiences. Consistent with the contact status, in some Christian circles, racial color-blind ideology is perceived as congruent with genuine Christian faith. In a qualitative study of White Christians, Mehta, Schneider, and Ecklund report that some participants viewed God as a color-blind entity and therefore viewed the correct Christian approach to racial relations as ignoring racial differences. As such, some participants from the study even viewed conversations

13. Helms, "Update of Helm's White and People of Color Racial Identity Models," 185.

14. Helms, *Black and White Racial Identity*, 55–58.

about race and racism as antithetical to what the church should be about.[15] For those in the contact status, any suggestion that racism plays a role in individual and communal suffering might be met with a dismissal or alternative explanations.

Famous Christian pastor and leader Franklin Graham posted the following statement on Facebook during a time when there were intense conversations and unrest across the nation about police shootings of Black men:

> Listen up—Blacks, Whites, Latinos, and everybody else. Most police shootings can be avoided. It comes down to respect for authority and obedience. If a police officer tells you to stop, you stop. If a police officer tells you to put your hands in the air, you put your hands in the air. If a police officer tells you to lay down face first with your hands behind your back, you lay down face first with your hands behind your back. It's as simple as that. Even if you think the police officer is wrong—YOU OBEY. Parents, teach your children to respect and obey those in authority.[16]

Note how this social media post asserts that racial disparity (in this case, disparity in how police might treat you in light of your racial background) can be resolved through the modification of individual behavior (e.g., obedience). What it does not do is acknowledge that bias might be internalized in structural ways and manifested through violence, including through law enforcement. This social media post triggered a response from Jim Wallis, who implored Franklin Graham to broaden his understanding of racism to include structural aspects "deeply embedded in our American society."[17]

15. Mehta et al., "'God Sees No Color,'" 629–39.

16. Franklin Graham, Facebook, March 12, 2015, https://www.facebook.com/FranklinGraham/posts/883361438386705.

17. Jim Wallis, "Last Thursday, Franklin Graham posted the following on Facebook," Facebook, March 16, 2015, https://www.facebook.com/permalink.php/?story_fbid=10152653035032441&id=207206302440. For more on Graham's post and Wallis's and others' responses, see Wallis, *America's Original Sin*, 53.

The next status is *disintegration*.[18] In this status, the White individual feels psychological discomfort because of increased awareness about race and related experiences. More than once in my teaching career I have had intense, emotional interactions with White students despairing about their identity. The most memorable incident was when a student slipped a handwritten note to me after a class discussion about White identity. Her note contained a poem vividly depicting her sense of disdain for her European heritage. In light of the WRIDM, the student was likely experiencing guilt and shame around her White identity because of learning about historical and contemporary forms of racism—emotional pains that feel incredibly uncomfortable.

Similarly, Christian writer and pastor Daniel Hill writes in his book *White Awake* that a foundational understanding of racism for White folks begins with the *awareness* of racism: "If we are to be liberated from blindness and to move toward greater levels of awakening, we must find a way to see the deeper meaning behind our daily encounters with race."[19]

The third status is *reintegration*.[20] In this status, there is a basic acknowledgment that what it means to be White is different from what it means to be a person of color in the US. At the same time, there is also a sense of hierarchy that perceives people of color as inferior to Whites and the ways of non-White communities as inferior to the ways of White communities. There might be minimal contact with people outside their own White social circles and instead the perpetuation of ideas about communities of color by those who hold similar thoughts. For example, a compelling study published in 2004 revealed that those with White-sounding names on job applications were much more likely to get interview invitations than applicants with Black-sounding names.[21] In connection to the reintegration status, the preference of a White name

18. Helms, *Black and White Racial Identity*, 58–60.
19. Hill, *White Awake*, 49.
20. Helms, *Black and White Racial Identity*, 60–61.
21. Bertrand and Mullainathan, "Are Emily and Greg More Employable," 997–99.

over a Black name reflects the belief that White culture is superior to Black culture.

Next, the White individual enters the *pseudo-independence* status.[22] Helms asserts that a person in this status has acquired an understanding of some of the disparities that exist between White communities and communities of color. Put simply, the validity of racism and its consequences are acknowledged. At the same time, the individual also believes that the antidote to racism is for people of color to change. That is, the focus of individual and societal efforts to eradicate racism should be to figure out how people of color can do "better."

Earlier in the book, I shared that I grew up as a Korean MK in the Philippines. My main community while living in the Philippines was my MK/international school community. In this private Christian school setting, I witnessed troubling instances of the "White savior" complex among my White peers, their parents, and teachers. I heard explicit and implicit disparaging remarks about the Filipina/o and other non-White cultures that made up our community. Moreover, I am ashamed to say, at times I, too, participated in looking down on non-White cultures.

The penultimate status is called *immersion-emersion*.[23] In contrast to the previous status, the person's emphasis in this status is on interrogating their own White identity and its role in a setting like the US. The focus is on learning more about the history of Whites and on learning from and about individuals who have made a positive journey of their own racial exploration. There is an understanding that the true solution to racism lies in those who hold more power. Therefore, the burden for antiracist work disproportionately falls on Whites, and there is a full embracing of that reality.

In the critically acclaimed film *The Color of Fear*, directed by Lee Mun Wah, several men converse with one another about race,

22. Helms, *Black and White Racial Identity*, 61–62.
23. Helms, *Black and White Racial Identity*, 62.

racism, White identity, and so on. At the end of the film, one of the characters, Hugh, looks directly into the camera to address White viewers and implores them to do their part in eradicating racism instead of relying on people of color to do the work.[24] In this articulation of the importance of White individuals and communities in dismantling racism, I contend that he is capturing the essence of what the immersion-emersion status emphasizes as an important aspect of White identity development.

When I reflect on this specific status of the WRIDM from a Christian faith perspective, I am again reminded how powerful and healing the posture of humility is. That is, individuals who have internalized a superficial understanding of racism (read: pseudo-independence) might accept the validity of the evil of racism, but they might also utilize an individualistic framework to place blame on individuals and communities of color for their marginalized experiences. In contrast, a healthy White identity recognizes the larger picture of structural contributions, contributions that are beyond individual control, to understand the stressors faced by communities of color. Such an understanding and posture require deep humility.

Related, the lack of defensiveness when difficult conversations about White identity take place, on topics such as White supremacy, is an important distinguishing aspect of the immersion-emersion status. Daniel Hill writes that "to no longer be defensive about white supremacy is a significant mark in the journey of blindness-to-sight and toward cultural identity development. It means you see the distinction between your worth and value as someone created in the image of God as well as the false set of values ascribed to you (and others) by white supremacy."[25] Similarly, Jim Wallis asserts that "if whites have profited from a racist system, we must try to change it. To go along with racist institutions and structures such as the racialized criminal justice system,

24. Lee Mun Wah, dir., *The Color of Fear* (StirFry Seminars, 1994), DVD, 1:21:15.
25. Hill, *White Awake*, 149.

to obliviously accept the economic order as it is, and to just quietly go about our personal business within institutional racism is to participate in white racism."[26]

The final status of the WRIDM in Helms's model is *autonomy*.[27] In this status, the individual continues to deepen a healthy sense of what Whiteness means. The status moves away from a rigid identity to a more flexible one that is open to learning new things. Moreover, the exploration of White identity naturally allows the exploration of other identities, and the lessons from the White identity exploration might be applied in other areas, such as sexism and other types of isms.

Again, I turn to Daniel Hill's book *White Awake*. Much of his final chapter on what it means to be an active participant in the work of racial justice echoes the most critical developments that take place in the autonomy status.[28] For instance, Hill argues that the White individual must deliberately connect with both people of color and White folks about their White identity. For connecting with people of color, Hill suggests that White individuals intentionally find themselves being led by people of color.[29] For connecting with fellow Whites, Hill urges persistence in working to educate one's own White communities and help them explore the meaning of Whiteness: "It may not seem like the most enticing work, but engaging with the white people in our extended community is one of the most concrete ways to make a difference. The apathy, indifference, and even hatred in the white community are the chief threats to racial progress in our country, and any little spark we can ignite is positive for the movement as a whole."[30]

In addition, the autonomy status is characterized by a willingness to be an ally to those from marginalized communities. Being

26. Wallis, *America's Original Sin*, 49.
27. Helms, *Black and White Racial Identity*, 62, 66.
28. Hill, *White Awake*, 161–83.
29. Hill, *White Awake*, 172–73.
30. Hill, *White Awake*, 175.

an ally has many facets, but a fundamental aspect of allyship is the act of listening to others. Jim Wallis recounts the story of a gathering in which a Black mother shared her deep fears about the physical safety of her son when he is in the presence of law enforcement. A White mother who heard about this fear—a fear that she could not fully relate to—simply *believed* her.[31] Derald Wing Sue describes this as the recognition of *experiential reality*, when those who learn about experiences of marginalized individuals respond with a posture of validation, instead of dismissing or invalidating the experiences.[32]

This famous quote from Dietrich Bonhoeffer captures the importance of listening to others as a Christian discipline: "The first service that one owes to others in the fellowship consists in listening to them. Just as love to God begins with listening to His Word, so the beginning of love . . . is learning to listen to them."[33]

Pause to Reflect

If You Identify as a White Person

Do you feel like this model adequately captures your experiences as a White person in the US? Why or why not? What are the positives of a model like this? Potential pitfalls?

Some Critique: Cultural Identity Development Models

It is intuitive to think about identity development in a linear fashion, progressing from one stage to another. Psychology is a descriptive discipline, interested in describing human emotions, thoughts, and behaviors using succinct frameworks and models. Given this, it is not surprising that linear models of cultural

31. Wallis, *America's Original Sin*, 196.
32. D. Sue, "Microaggressions and 'Evidence,'" 170–71.
33. Bonhoeffer, *Life Together*, 97.

development are the most popular among psychological studies focused on cultural identity development.

But my guess is that as you were reading over the descriptions of the major identity development models, some questions formed in your mind that parallel the major critiques of the models in psychological science.[34] First, identity development models tend to treat identities as detached from one another.[35] Note that the identity models described earlier are entirely focused on one dimension of culture—namely, race and ethnicity. But identities develop in connection to other identities. As noted earlier, Kimberlé Crenshaw coined the term "intersectionality" to capture the idea that in real life, multiple identities (e.g., gender and race) are in a dynamic relationship with one another to shape experiences and perspectives.[36] For example, even though I share my racial identity with my female Asian American colleagues, their experiences as Asian American women might look different from my experiences as an Asian American man. A study of female professors teaching at Christian universities found some clear examples of discrimination that included both racial and gender considerations, such as unfair questions about qualifications due to race or gender.[37] Many popular identity development models fall short because they do not adequately consider intersectionality.

Second, the linear progression typically captured in major identity development models is unrealistic.[38] That is, there is an assumption that people progress neatly through these statuses or stages, and there is a lack of attention on the possibility of a return to an earlier stage.[39] Moreover, there is a bias toward

34. For a more comprehensive critique, see Mio et al., *Multicultural Psychology*, 280–81.
35. Holvino, "'Simultaneity' of Identities," 164.
36. Crenshaw, "Mapping the Margins."
37. C. Kim et al., "Coping with Discrimination in Academia," 295–96.
38. Rowe et al., "White Racial Identity Models," 130–33.
39. Parham, "Cycles of Psychological Nigrescence," 195.

viewing the final stage as the most ideal outcome for the mental health of the individual.[40]

Now, to be clear, as I reflected about the WRIDM earlier, there is a compelling case that the latter statuses or stages reflect more faithful Christian living, such as the connection I made between humility and the immersion-emersion status. I would argue that espousing the actions and values of a more developed stage can result in the ability to love those from other cultures more deeply and faithfully.

At the same time, this belief that we are being transformed into a deeper knowledge of our own and others' identities should be held in balance with the "come as you are" message of Christianity. For example, individuals who are in the contact status of the WRIDM should not be dismissed or looked down on but instead recognized as people shaped by their own experiences in life (e.g., not having had many interactions with non-White individuals). Their racially color-blind approach might be misguided in the sense that it invalidates the diverse experiences of communities of color, but it is likely that they are genuine in espousing such a view (e.g., a theological conviction that we should not pay attention to race when interacting with others). Again, as someone who studies the psychological harm that a racial color blindness can inflict, I find it challenging to hold these thoughts in tension. But I do believe that a healthy Christian community should seek to recognize that a range of beliefs about identity exists among us, while clearly articulating the truth that there are more loving and validating ways to speak about identity.

Key Takeaways

1. Congruent with classic developmental theories, cultural identity development includes both an exploration and a commitment to an identity.

40. Barker-Hackett, "African Americans in the New Millennium," 124.

2. Comprehensive models like D. Sue and Sue's R/CID can capture the identity development of individuals from different racial and cultural groups, while culture-specific models describe the identity development within a cultural or racial group (e.g., Cross's Nigrescence model, Helms's WRIDM).
3. The WRIDM, in particular, offers many entry points for White Christians to reflect on their own identities as White people in the US context.
4. Stage models of cultural identity development, while intuitive, can falsely convey that identity develops in a linear manner.

Activities and Discussion Questions

1. Create your own identity development model.
   a. Select a cultural identity to reflect on. It might be most straightforward to select *one* domain.
   b. Create or describe a stage model that depicts your identity in the domain that you chose. Try to include at least four stages. For each stage, respond to the following questions: (i) What would you call the stage? (ii) What are the key features of this stage, especially regarding your own feelings and perspectives about your own identity? (iii) How did you feel about or behave toward other people from a different identity group? How did you treat the members of your own group? Tell stories illustrating each stage.
   c. How did your faith community (or communities) influence your progression through these stages?
   d. Are there concrete things that you can do *today* to further explore your identity? Further commit?
   e. Alternatively, create a nonlinear description of your identity development. Write and reflect on the ways in which

different circumstances in your life have shaped who you are today in a particular identity development.

2. Find an identity model development described in the literature. What did it do well? What did it not do well? What kind of faith or religious variables might it also examine?

Case Study

Isabella is a Mexican American college student who is currently enrolled in a public university in the Midwest US. Although she is an American citizen by birth, she has lived most of her life outside the US as a child of military parents. She has lived in Japan, South Korea, and Germany. As such, she has experienced multiple influences on her ethnic and racial identity, including her Mexican culture, American culture, and the global cultures that she was a part of while growing up. When her therapist asks her to articulate the development of her cultural identity, she is unsure how to go about processing this. Moreover, she joined a church community, thinking that there would be an opportunity to practice her faith in a community of believers supportive of the complexities of her identity and experiences. To her disappointment, although the church community has been warm and kind, the people are generally unsure how to respond when she shares her diverse experiences and struggles.

1. What support networks might be helpful for Isabella to explore her identity?
2. How might a faith community be helpful in identity exploration? How might it hurt?
3. How might the intersectionality perspective be helpful for others to understand Isabella? For Isabella to understand her own identity?

6

Loving the Sojourners

Acculturation

> Achieng is an international undergraduate student from Kenya studying at a small liberal arts Christian college located in South Carolina. Although she enjoys many different kinds of American food (but certainly not all) and even follows a few American TV shows (to be able to have casual conversations about them with her friends and roommates), Achieng feels that, at times, she just does not fully grasp the cultural values and beliefs of her American peers. In fact, she sometimes feels like her values and beliefs are at odds with her American counterparts, even though they share the common identity of being Christian.

Acculturation is one of the most widely studied cultural constructs in multicultural and cross-cultural psychology. A classic definition of "acculturation" is "those phenomena which result when groups of individuals having different cultures come into continuous first-hand contact, with subsequent changes in the original cultural patterns of either or both groups."[1]

1. Redfield et al., "Memorandum for the Study of Acculturation," 149.

This popular definition points to some fundamental aspects of acculturation. First, acculturation cannot occur without interpersonal contact with those from a different culture; one does not acculturate to the ways of a different country, for example, by passively watching YouTube videos or listening to podcasts about the country. Second, acculturation must include *changes*. If interpersonal contact with a different culture occurs but no meaningful changes result, then the person cannot be described as having acculturated. Third, notice the word "patterns" in the definition, with the emphasis on the plural; acculturation theory and research recognize that meaningful changes occur across multiple dimensions, whether internal or external. I will elaborate more on the multidimensionality of acculturation later in this chapter. Finally, it should be noted that although much of the research focuses on the experiences of those who are doing the acculturating (e.g., immigrants), acculturation also affects those who are part of the host culture that welcomes or does not welcome them. Again, I will elaborate on this point later, especially in connection to the implications for Christian living. Next, I would like to respond to some important queries about acculturation in psychological science.

Loss of One = Gain of Another?

One aspect that the above definition does not fully capture is the *bilinear* characteristic of acculturation. A unilinear conceptualization of acculturation argues that as people acquire a different culture, they lose their culture of origin.[2] Although this conceptualization might be applied in some research situations and is used in our everyday language (e.g., describing an immigrant or a person of color who has distanced themselves from their culture of origin as "acculturated"), scholars now recognize that a more accurate and fuller understanding of acculturation should involve

2. E. Yoon et al., "Meta-Analysis of Acculturation," 343.

examination of not only adaptation to the new setting but also the socialization into and the retention of one's culture of origin. Commonly, the term "enculturation" is used to describe this process.[3] To reiterate the important lesson here, acculturation is best described as a combination of adaptation to the host culture and adherence to the original one.

The Acculturation Rating Scale for Mexican Americans-II (ARSMA-II) is a good example of a bilinear measure of acculturation; it assesses orientation among Mexican Americans toward Mexican and European American cultures.[4] As such, in the ARSMA-II, both acculturation and enculturation are assessed (e.g., affinity for entertainment in both English and Spanish).[5]

John Berry's acculturation strategies framework is based on this bilinear assumption and is widely cited in acculturation research.[6] Describing how one might choose to acculturate to a new context, Berry argues that there are two fundamental questions: (1) What is the level of affinity toward or endorsement of the host culture? (2) What is the level of adherence to the culture of origin? Depending on how one answers these questions (high or low), four possible acculturation strategies can result:[7]

Marginalization: disconnected from both culture of origin and host culture; that is, low on both cultures.

Separation: more emphasis on connecting to the culture of origin and less emphasis on learning about the host culture; that is, low on host culture and high on culture of origin.

Assimilation: more emphasis on learning the new culture and less willingness to stay connected to the culture of origin; that is, low on culture of origin and high on host culture.

3. B. Kim, "Acculturation and Enculturation," 142–43.
4. Cuéllar et al., "Acculturation Rating Scale," 275–304.
5. Cuéllar et al., "Acculturation Rating Scale," 297.
6. Berry, "Lead Article," 9–12.
7. Berry, "Lead Article," 9–10.

Integration or biculturalism: a balanced approach that values connections to both culture of origin and host culture; that is, high on both cultures.

As one might expect, a plethora of research examines how these acculturation strategies might affect well-being. To simplify a very complicated process, the research essentially asks which acculturation strategy tends to be affiliated with the best adjustment. Integration or biculturalism is most frequently cited as the strategy that is most adaptive.[8]

Does Acculturation Happen Externally or Internally?

Earlier in this chapter I pointed out that acculturation can occur across multiple domains of a person's life. Scholars refer to this as a *multidimensional* understanding of acculturation.[9] The most obvious aspects of acculturation, one might argue, are the observable cultural changes or retentions—or *behaviors*. "Behavioral acculturation" can refer to languages that one is able to speak, food that one most regularly consumes, or types of friendships pursued.[10] As you can guess, behavioral acculturation tends to be really popular not only in popular culture but also in psychological research, given how it is readily observable.

In the Asian American context, some scholars use the Asian American Multidimensional Acculturation Scale (AAMAS).[11] Most of the items on this scale tap into the external or behavioral aspects of acculturation (e.g., reading and writing ability, affinity for food).[12] Like ARSMA-II, this measure asks participants to

8. Nguyen and Benet-Martínez, "Biculturalism and Adjustment," 131.

9. For examples, see Abraído-Lanza et al., "Toward a Theory-Driven Model," 1343; Wallace et al., "Review of Acculturation Measures," 49; Miller, "Bilinear Multidimensional Measurement," 120.

10. B. Kim and Omizo, "Behavioral Acculturation and Enculturation," 246.

11. Gim Chung et al., "Asian American Multidimensional Acculturation," 66–80.

12. Gim Chung et al., "Asian American Multidimensional Acculturation," 73–74.

consider different cultural groups (e.g., one's own Asian ethnic group, other Asian groups, and White mainstream groups) when answering each question.[13]

But because there are internal aspects of culture (see chap. 1, where I provide definitions of "culture"), changes in culture can also take place internally. Notably, acculturation can affect one's cultural values and sense of self.[14] For instance, acculturation to the US context might mean that an individual increasingly embraces cultural values that are ingrained in American culture (e.g., emphasis on an independent understanding of the self).[15] Can you think of any "American" values that you might have been socialized into?

Returning to the Asian American setting, research instruments that assess acculturation to the US context, as well as enculturation to Asian ones, are available in the psychological literature. The Asian American Values Scale–Multidimensional (AAVS-M) is a measure of socialization into core Asian cultural values, and it assesses several types of Asian values, such as family recognition through achievement and emotional self-control.[16] On the flip side, the European American Values Scale for Asian Americans–Revised (EAVS-AA-R) asks about the level that Asian Americans embrace mainstream American culture in such areas as child-rearing and marital relationships to measure acculturation to certain mainstream American cultural values.[17]

One important lesson, then, in thinking about acculturation is that we should not draw firm conclusions about one's acculturation and enculturation levels on the basis of how one comes across behaviorally or externally. Indeed, research suggests that

13. Gim Chung et al., "Asian American Multidimensional Acculturation," 68.

14. Abe-Kim et al., "Unidimensional Versus Multidimensional Approaches," 241–43.

15. Markus and Kitayama, "Culture and the Self," 226–29.

16. For complete list of values included in the measure, see B. Kim et al., "Asian American Values Scale," 192–93.

17. S. Hong et al., "Psychometric Revision of the European American Values Scale," 202.

behavioral acculturation tends to occur faster than value acculturation.[18] Even though someone may seem acculturated externally, that person and the host culture may not value the same things.

This caution against making assumptions about someone's internal acculturation level reminds me of 1 Samuel 16:7: "But the Lord said to Samuel, 'Do not consider his appearance or his height, for I have rejected him. The Lord does not look at the things people look at. People look at the outward appearance, but the Lord looks at the heart.'" I appreciate this passage because it points to the importance of recognizing and seeing the whole person—not just the external but the internal as well.

What Psychological Outcomes Are Possible Due to Acculturation?

When acculturation becomes stressful, one might use the term "acculturative stress" to describe the experience, which can manifest in a variety of ways.[19] For example, a measure of international students' acculturative stress captures things like loneliness, feelings of guilt, and experiences of discrimination.[20] Likewise, Achieng's story in the beginning of the chapter captures some of these acculturative stressors. Of course, it should be noted that not all who experience migration, such as international students, experience acculturative stress, but for those who do, acculturative stress is associated with deleterious outcomes, such as lower interpersonal connectedness.[21] The counterpart to acculturative stress might be described as adaptation or adjustment. "Sociocultural adaptation" describes the "cultural competencies acquired by sojourners and new immigrants during cross-cultural transition."[22] For ex-

18. E. Yoon et al., "Meta-Analysis of Acculturation," 362.
19. Berry, "Lead Article," 19.
20. Sandhu and Asrabadi, "Development of an Acculturative Stress Scale," 443.
21. Koo et al., "First Year of Acculturation," 286–88.
22. Wilson et al., "Measuring Cultural Competencies," 1476.

ample, the Revised Sociocultural Adaptation Scale asks migrants about their perceived level of competence in things like speaking and writing the new language, interacting with people of the new culture, and navigating their new host culture.[23]

Is Acculturation Voluntary or Involuntary?

It is important to understand that acculturation is not a purely voluntary process. The phrase "acculturation strategy" implies that there is a volitional aspect of acculturation, that one can freely choose a certain approach to acculturation. But in reality, some people might be forced or pressured into certain types of acculturation experiences. International students can be described as academic sojourners—those who are temporarily traveling to the US, for example, without the long-term goal of settling into the country. Those who have long-term goals of settling into a new country like the United States might be described as immigrants. Both international students and immigrants are examples of folks who have voluntarily relocated to a different country or culture. As such, their approach to acculturation might also have substantive voluntary elements. In contrast, there are those who are on the move as refugees or asylum seekers. Their acculturative experiences might be described as involuntary.

In the face of the American hyperindividualism and the myth of meritocracy that permeate our culture, we are prone to thinking that everyone who migrates to the US will have the same opportunities available to them, without any structural barriers getting in the way of their success. As noted in chapter 1, Emerson and Smith provide compelling data that the White evangelical church in the US can be especially susceptible to such forms of individualism.[24] Such an individualistic approach can interfere with empathizing with the difficulties that migrating groups might experience.

23. Wilson et al., "Measuring Cultural Competencies," 1484.
24. Emerson and Smith, *Divided by Faith*.

Instead, understanding the role of the hosts—those who typically have more resources than the migrants—in the successful adaptation of migrants is important. From a Christian perspective, one way to obey the biblical commands directed toward those who are hosts is to love the foreigners among us (Lev. 19:34). Psychological science says that the attitudes of the hosts and the societal structures reflecting these attitudes are impactful in helping migrants acculturate successfully. For example, in response to Berry's model of acculturation strategies, it has been argued that there must be a match between the acculturation strategy utilized by the migrating individual and the attitudes of those in the host culture.[25] In other words, how a society is structured is important in realizing the full potential of a particular acculturation strategy. If a country's immigration policies and attitudes are all about helping migrants *assimilate* into the mainstream culture, then there will be intentional efforts to assist migrants in being fully absorbed into the mainstream culture. Likewise, a *bicultural* emphasis might be present, an emphasis on retaining one's original culture even while adapting to the new one.

Pause to Reflect

In your assessment, how would you describe *your* society's stance toward migrants?

Does Religion Help or Hurt?

Given the relevance of the attitudes of the host culture in the acculturation process, it is not surprising that psychological science has asked what the role of religion is in shaping people's attitudes toward migrants and their experiences. As with many research findings in the psychology of religion literature, the answer is

25. Bourhis et al., "Towards an Interactive Acculturation Model," 369–84.

complicated. On the one hand, some studies suggest that religion might foster unfavorable views of migrating individuals. For example, people who expressed anti-immigrant attitudes were more likely to be Christians than non-Christians.[26] Similarly, Christians were more likely than irreligious people to express support for separating immigrant families.[27]

A deeper dive into the empirical evidence, however, provides a more nuanced insight into how religion can form attitudes toward migrants. A *particular* type of religiosity might predict anti-immigrant attitudes. For example, beyond the influence of religion, cultural humility was predictive of favorable views about Syrian refugees.[28] This suggests that it is not religion across the board that feeds into unfavorable attitudes but instead some of the specific ways that religion might be applied and practiced. An important implication for those who advocate for change in immigration views, whether in the public or the private sphere, is to "seek to strengthen the existing moral foundations of care and fairness in those that they seek to influence, rather than attempting to change political views."[29]

In sum, for those who are welcoming migrants into their culture, religion can serve as a barrier or a facilitator.

Religion as a Coping Strategy

For religious folks, spirituality can provide valuable resources for making sense of or responding to difficulties associated with transitioning to a new culture. As I briefly mentioned in chapter 1, "religious coping" refers to the reliance on the sacred for coping, and a popular conceptualization bifurcates coping into positive religious coping (e.g., benevolent religious reappraisal or the rethinking of the difficult situation in light of one's spirituality)

26. Disney, "Associations Between Humanitarianism, Othering, and Religious Affiliation," 65–68.

27. Rowatt et al., "Attitudes Toward Separating," 122–24.

28. Captari et al., "Prejudicial and Welcoming Attitudes," 130–32.

29. Captari et al., "Prejudicial and Welcoming Attitudes," 135.

and negative religious coping (e.g., a punishing-God reappraisal or a reformulation of the challenging situation as a form of punishment for one's wrongdoing).[30] In general, positive religious coping is associated with favorable adjustment outcomes, and negative religious coping is associated with unfavorable adjustment outcomes.[31]

Studies, especially narrative or qualitative studies, have suggested that religion can help migrants better cope with the stressors of the migration experience. A qualitative study of fifteen Chinese Christian migrants in Ireland reported that the Christian religion served to provide folks with a coping strategy in response to various acculturative stressors (e.g., discrimination), in addition to providing a source of spiritual satisfaction.[32] As such, religion facilitated well-being against the backdrop of acculturative stressors in a compelling way. For instance, some participants reported that they were able to overcome the sting of overt discrimination through prayers and relationship with God.[33] Likewise, in a qualitative study of twelve international students in the US, religious strategies and practices utilized by religious participants for coping with acculturative stress resulted in improved outcomes across domains, such as academic performance.[34] It should be noted that this study focused on religion overall, not just the Christian religion.

In sum, religion for those who are experiencing acculturative stress can be helpful. But can religion also help those who might have experienced significant migration trauma, such as asylum seekers and refugees?

Migration, Meaning, and Post-Traumatic Growth

"Post-traumatic growth" describes the experiences of folks who emerge out of a challenging experience with a transformed view

30. Pargament et al., "Many Methods of Religious Coping," 522–25.
31. Pargament et al., "Many Methods of Religious Coping," 524–25.
32. Zhu, "Personal Mental Impacts of Christian Faith," 451–57.
33. Zhu, "Personal Mental Impacts of Christian Faith," 453–54.
34. Philip et al., "Impact of Religion/Spirituality," 29–36.

of self, relationships, and life.[35] Given religion's focus on helping individuals make meaning, it is not surprising that religion tends to be correlated with post-traumatic growth, including for those who have experienced migration trauma. In a sample of Syrian refugees in Turkey, the religiosity of the participants was associated with post-traumatic growth.[36] Similarly, a qualitative study of asylum seekers and refugees in the United Kingdom found that social support afforded through religion was an important consideration for the post-traumatic growth of the participants.[37] Powerfully, a study with a large sample of adult survivors of traumatic experiences who were recruited from a faith setting in Liberia and from a Liberian refugee camp in Ghana reported that *forgiveness* was an important consideration in how religious coping was related to post-traumatic growth.[38]

What drives post-traumatic growth for those who have experienced migration trauma might be active meaning making. "Meaning making" refers to the psychological process of making sense of challenging life experiences in a way that leads to better psychological health.[39] In the Bible, a prime example of meaning making through forgiveness, and ultimately post-traumatic growth, is the well-known Old Testament story of Joseph.

Joseph endured much trauma, including the trauma of forcibly being taken across borders because he was sold by his own siblings to a land distant from home. In today's language, we might say that he was trafficked across borders—the ultimate form of involuntary migration. Indeed, he experienced acculturative stress—before and during migration—through one devastating incident after another.

This is what I wrote about Joseph's experiences in a *Psychology Today* blog post:

35. Tedeschi and Calhoun, "Posttraumatic Growth Inventory," 458.
36. Ersahin, "Post-Traumatic Growth Among Syrian Refugees," 2402–3.
37. Taylor et al., "Loss, Grief, and Growth," 109–10.
38. Ochu et al., "Religious Coping, Dispositional Forgiveness," 107–12.
39. C. Park, "Making Sense of the Meaning Literature," 257–62.

- His own brothers, initially plotting to murder him, instead sold him away as a slave (Genesis 37:18–36).
- While working as a servant, Joseph was falsely accused of sexual assault by his master's wife after he rejected her advances. As a result, he was thrown into prison for a crime he did not commit (Genesis 39:1–20).
- While in prison, he accurately interpreted the dream of a fellow inmate, who was Pharaoh's cupbearer. Among other things, Joseph predicted that the cupbearer would be restored to his position. Joseph asked him to put in a good word on his behalf when he was freed from jail, but the cupbearer forgot about Joseph once he was released (Genesis 40:9–23).[40]

And this is not even an exhaustive list of all the significant difficulties that Joseph endured in his life.

Skip ahead to Joseph's moment of reunion with his brothers after many years of separation. Now Joseph is in one of the most powerful positions possible; his brothers, when they realize that they are in the presence of the sibling whom they literally tried to kill many years ago, tremble in fear.

The traumatic nature of Joseph's experiences makes his dramatic declaration of forgiveness and meaning making to his brothers that much more shocking: "But Joseph said to them, 'Do not fear, for am I in the place of God? As for you, you meant evil against me, but God meant it for good, to bring it about that many people should be kept alive, as they are today. So do not fear; I will provide for you and your little ones.' Thus he comforted them and spoke kindly to them" (Gen. 50:19–21 ESV).[41] If I were Joseph, faced with this encounter with my brothers after many years, I would have liked to utter so many

40. P. Kim, "'God Meant It.'"

41. I quote the ESV here because of the contrast between "meant evil" and "meant it for good."

other things to my siblings: *What were you thinking when you sold me? How do you like me now? You are going to get what you deserve—this is a moment of justice that God has brought in front of me.* Instead, Joseph turns to his brothers and shares the meaning making that he has landed on: *You did bad things, but God was working for the greater good all along*. And he reassures them that he will not deliver vengeance on them. What a powerful moment of forgiveness and meaning making stemming from a deep faith in God.

This is a good moment to interject this important caveat: Pressuring victims of injustice to prematurely forgive those who did them wrong is, of course, deeply problematic. Wilco De Vries warns against the dangers of forcing forgiveness on those who have experienced abuse, referring to it as a "silencing technique" used in some Christian contexts.[42] Indeed, when I point to Joseph's words and actions toward his brothers as a good thing in connection with meaning making for traumatic cross-cultural experiences, I am certainly not saying that every migrant who has experienced trauma should default to automatic and immediate forgiveness. I deeply recognize the exacerbation of problems and hurts that coercive and premature forgiveness in the name of Christianity can cause for folks who have been hurt by interpersonal or structural wrongdoings.

But an uncoerced, volitional act of extending forgiveness within a larger meaning-making process can be a powerful psychological tool.

A study of Syrian refugees living in Portugal describes several meaning-making processes; an especially important process for the refugees was searching for meaning as a community of people, which allowed collective questions (e.g., "Why us?") to be asked in relation to the war and resettlement.[43] The same study reports that collectively for these religious participants (the majority of whom

42. De Vries, "Danger of Forcing Forgiveness."
43. Matos et al., "'War Made Me a Better Person,'" 7–9.

were Muslim), meaning making through asking deep questions about life was an important process.[44]

Finally, it should be noted that the same study argues that these processes of meaning making did not stop at exploration; rather, there were outcomes such as a sense of peace and the perception that they experienced growth.[45] Similarly, in a sample of resettled Karen refugees, all of whom identified as Christian, Christian religion and various functions of Christian religion (e.g., community attached to religion and praying to God in the face of difficult situations) all served to help the refugees make sense of the difficult migration experience.[46] Likewise, in a study of Congolese refugees and asylum seekers in Johannesburg, South Africa, forgiveness was an important stance that contributed to their well-being.[47]

Pause to Reflect

What would it look like for faith communities to help create and maintain an environment that facilitates meaning making for migrants?

I hope that some of the reflections, especially in the latter part of this chapter, are coming across clearly in their purpose—namely, that taking care of migrants is a critical part of the Christian mandate to love our neighbors. The psychological science reviewed in this chapter only reinforces this perspective.

Torli H. Krua writes important words that I would like to use in closing this chapter on acculturation and enculturation. Christian hosts (e.g., Americans who are Christian) need to keep in mind some profound principles when welcoming migrants to our communities in a collaborative relationship with immigrant leaders: "This will include things like taking a genuine interest in the stories, issues,

44. Matos et al., "'War Made Me a Better Person,'" 7–11.
45. Matos et al., "'War Made Me a Better Person,'" 12–13.
46. Muruthi et al., "'We Pray as a Family,'" 1731–34.
47. Kandemiri, "Forgiveness as a Positive," 1053.

history, and struggles of refugees; respecting and deferring to refugee leadership; and loving all refugees, Christian and non-Christian."[48]

Key Takeaways

1. "Acculturation" describes changes that occur due to a person experiencing a different culture.
2. A *bilinear* understanding of acculturation, which considers both the culture of origin and the new culture (host culture), is the best approach.
3. Acculturation can occur externally (e.g., behaviors) or internally (e.g., values and beliefs).
4. When acculturation is difficult, stressful outcomes can result, referred to as "acculturative stress."
5. People who are on the "other side of acculturation" (i.e., the host culture) can do their part in welcoming those who are acculturating.
6. Christian faith can shape both unfavorable and favorable attitudes toward immigrants.
7. Christian faith can help protect against the negative effects of acculturative stress.
8. Meaning making is an example of how those who have experienced migration trauma can start to make sense of their experiences, including from a Christian faith perspective.

Activities and Discussion Questions

1. Have you ever experienced living in a culture different from your own for a significant amount of time? What factors

48. Krua, "Evangelism That Reconciles," 121.

were helpful to your acculturation process? What factors were not as helpful, or perhaps even hurtful, in the adjustment to a new culture?

2. Now think about a time when you were part of the host culture. What did you do that was helpful? Not as helpful? How can you encourage your communities, including faith communities, to do better in terms of hosting those who are migrating?
3. The reminder about the importance of the host culture in the whole process of acculturation prompts the question, What posture does your Christian community display toward those who are migrating? What is the posture that we as a Christian community should aspire toward?
4. Look up an article that highlights a religious factor that can be facilitative for the well-being of migrants. Also look up an article that highlights a religious factor that can be destructive to the well-being of migrants.
5. Conduct a database search of measures of acculturation, enculturation, or sociocultural adaptation. Try to find a measure that is valid for use in light of your own cultural identities. Fill out the measure and reflect on your scores. Do you feel like the measure items adequately capture your own acculturative experiences? Why or why not?

Case Study

Pablo is a high school senior. He resides in Los Angeles, California, with his parents, who immigrated from Mexico when Pablo was eight years old. Because Pablo is the only person in the family who speaks English well, he helps his father with his landscaping business. He is in charge of communicating with his father's clients about scheduling, payments, and so on. At school, like a typical student, Pablo thrives in some classes and struggles in others. He is active in various extracurricular activities. He recognizes that he could be spending more time on schoolwork, but he has accepted the reality that he will have to sacrifice some of that time for the sake of the family business. He has made many American friends of various ethnicities. To any casual observer, Pablo appears well-adjusted to life in the US. But Pablo experiences internal struggles that he has told very few people about; he is unsure whom he might talk to about these things. The more he experiences American culture, the more Pablo realizes that his beliefs and values tend to conflict with mainstream American culture. For example, the other day at his church youth group, the youth pastor said during a sermon, "God desires that you prioritize your education and be in school. That's the act of worship that you must do as a high school student." Pablo couldn't help but wonder about his family situation and how his role in the family fits into this description of worship. Specifically, he feels as though what he is doing—serving his family, prioritizing family needs over individual ones—is something that is also honoring of God, but his church community does not seem to grasp its value.

1. Using Berry's acculturation strategies framework, how would you describe Pablo's acculturation?
2. How is enculturation playing a role in Pablo's current situation? That is, what are some values and beliefs that Pablo was socialized into that might be playing a role?
3. How can messages like "_______ is pleasing to God, and _______ is not" perpetuate the message of superiority of one culture over another?
4. How can the host culture and its members (e.g., his church community) facilitate better relational and inner health for people like Pablo?

7

The Self Makes a Difference

Emotions Across Cultures

> Blessed are those who mourn,
> for they will be comforted.
>
> —Matthew 5:4

Emotions are an integral part of what it means to be human. How are you feeling? Reflect on the feelings and underlying thoughts that you have experienced up to this point today; you can likely name a range of emotions and cognitions, and maybe a *wide* range of emotions if your day was like mine. Furthermore, certain emotions and related behaviors, like mourning in the verse above, can foster connections with other people. In this chapter, we will go deeper into how a culturally shaped understanding of the self can influence emotions. But let's first begin with an example of how emotions are generalizable across cultures.

Universality of Emotions

A well-known example of a shared (i.e., universal) aspect of emotions is their *expression* on the face. A classic study by Ekman and Friesen provides compelling evidence for the universality of certain feelings depicted on the face.[1] Ekman and Friesen recruited Fore people from the South East Highlands of New Guinea who had had minimal exposure to foreign faces.[2] For these research participants, the recognition of emotions on unfamiliar faces, compared to familiar ones, would be that much more compelling. In the study, participants were told stories and then were asked to identify the emotion conveyed in the story by selecting the correct facial expression depicted on a foreign face. The outcome variable, then, was the ability to accurately identify the feelings. In strong support for universality of emotion, the participants were able to identify most of the emotions correctly.[3]

So the concept of emotions is readily generalizable across cultures. It is no surprise, then, that a film like Pixar's *Inside Out* was a big hit globally.[4] The emotions portrayed in the film are relatable to children and adults across global contexts.

Culture-Specific Aspects of Emotions: Role of Independence and Interdependence

Let's stay on the topic of *Inside Out* and its global appeal for just a bit more. When the film was distributed internationally, some of the most memorable scenes had to be altered for non-US audiences due to equivalency issues. For instance, the depiction of broccoli as a trigger for disgust had to be altered in countries where broccoli is not despised by young children (imagine that!); likewise, the depiction of ice hockey was altered to soccer to make the sport more relatable to some viewers.[5]

1. Ekman and Friesen, "Constants Across Cultures."
2. Ekman and Friesen, "Constants Across Cultures," 125.
3. Ekman and Friesen, "Constants Across Cultures," 125–28.
4. Pete Docter, dir., *Inside Out* (Pixar Animation Studios, 2015), https://www.disneyplus.com/movies/inside-out/uzQ2ycVDi2IE.
5. Bradley, "*Inside Out* Director Pete Docter Explains."

Indeed, although the fundamental emotions might be generalizable across cultures, the triggers for those emotions, as well as the factors that contribute to the intensity and frequency of the emotions, might be shaped by cultural norms.

One cultural construct that is often discussed in psychology in relation to emotions is *self-construal*.[6] In a seminal article, Markus and Kitayama first define "independent self-construal" and "interdependent self-construal" and then expand on how the two types can influence our thoughts, drives, and most important to this chapter, *feelings*. "Independent self-construal" refers to an understanding of the self that is characterized by clear boundaries between the self and others; "interdependent self-construal" refers to an understanding of the self that is reliant on a person's connection with those who are part of their close social network. Put simply, independence emphasizes the distinctiveness of the individual, and interdependence emphasizes the person's interconnectedness.[7]

Markus and Kitayama argue that the cultural framework of interdependence and independence can shape the frequency and the acceptability of certain emotions.[8] Specifically, they write that *ego-focused* emotions strengthen the independent view of self.[9] Ego-focused emotions tend to primarily emphasize individual needs and goals. For instance, have you ever felt pride because of a personal accomplishment and expressed it in person or on social media? That outward expression of pride can be conceptualized as consistent with the goals of independent self-construal; the emotion permits the person to, at least for a few moments, distinguish themself from others. It advances the individual's needs. It separates the self from other people.

But there are emotions that are designed to promote the goals of an interdependent self-construal. Markus and Kitayama refer

6. Markus and Kitayama, "Culture and the Self."
7. Markus and Kitayama, "Culture and the Self," 225–29.
8. Markus and Kitayama, "Culture and the Self," 235–39.
9. Markus and Kitayama, "Culture and the Self," 235.

to these as *other-focused* emotions.[10] Have you ever felt guilty because you felt like you did not do your part in a group project? Chances are, guilt led you to make some concrete behavioral changes—to reach out to your group, volunteer to do more tasks, and even apologize for your inaction. As such, the emotion of guilt can cause an individual to be attuned to the larger social network and, when necessary, can lead an individual to address the needs of a group.

By the way, as I have been saying elsewhere in this book, both an interdependent and an independent understanding of the self are critical for the flourishing of individuals in communities. First Corinthians 12 is a well-known passage that speaks eloquently to the necessity of both in the body of Christ: "Just as a body, though one, has many parts, but all its many parts form one body, so it is with Christ. For we were all baptized by one Spirit so as to form one body—whether Jews or Gentiles, slave or free—and we were all given the one Spirit to drink. Even so the body is not made up of one part but of many" (vv. 12–14). A corollary of this powerful description of God's family, as including both independent and interdependent aspects, is that emotions addressing the goals of individuals and communities are a necessary part of faithful Christian living. First Corinthians 12:25–27 reads, "So that there should be no division in the body, but that its parts should have equal concern for each other. If one part suffers, every part suffers with it; if one part is honored, every part rejoices with it. Now you are the body of Christ, and each one of you is a part of it."

I am especially struck by how independence and interdependence are not dichotomized in this passage, as the field of psychology is sometimes prone to doing. Instead, independence and interdependence are recognized as necessary postures in Christian settings, including when individuals are experiencing and expressing emotions. I would argue that the statement "If one part suffers, every part suffers with it" speaks clearly to the notion that we are

10. Markus and Kitayama, "Culture and the Self," 235.

to recognize the validity of one person's emotion but also find ways to share the burden of that sadness; this sounds a lot like empathy. Put differently, what might have begun with an ego-focused emotion, such as an individual asserting their individuality and distinguishing themself from others by expressing sadness over their circumstances, can transform into an other-focused emotion of empathy if the community responds in a Christlike manner. Likewise, "if one part is honored"—which certainly sounds like pride for big accomplishments—is quickly followed by "every part rejoices"; this seems to assert that pride, as an ego-focused emotion, can be redeemed to include a collective celebration about the connection to others. Pride at the individual level is a normal human emotion, but its recognition by loved ones can result in a fuller experience of the Christian body. Again, this is an example of ego-focused and other-focused emotions coherently and beautifully coming together.

Pause to Reflect

Think about a time you felt a strong other-focused emotion. What was it, and what did it allow you to achieve? Can you think of how other-focused emotions might contribute to Christian flourishing? Hinder it? Now think about a time you felt a strong ego-focused emotion. What was it, and how did it serve you? Can you think of how ego-focused emotions might contribute to Christian flourishing? Hinder it?

Going Deeper with Anger

Let's talk about anger. As an ego-focused emotion, anger permits the individual to differentiate their identity from another person who has done wrong. Think about a time when you felt angry toward a family member or a friend. If you expressed that anger, your subconscious motivation was to psychologically distance yourself from that person, at least temporarily, as a way to communicate your indignation about what took place or what was said. From a cultural perspective, we might argue that expressed anger allows the assertion of the self in the presence of others. Put differently, in the moment that anger is expressed, there is a prioritizing or elevating of the self over another person.

If you are from a Christian background, you likely have heard many sermons and participated in many Bible studies about anger. Not surprisingly, there are many warnings or admonishments against anger in Christian traditions, especially in interpersonal relationships. That is, there is a recognition that the expression of anger deleteriously affects relational bonds. For instance, "A hot-tempered person must pay the penalty; rescue them, and you will have to do it again" (Prov. 19:19). And, "An angry person stirs up conflict, and a hot-tempered person commits many sins" (Prov. 29:22). So, certainly, anger is an emotion that can get in the way of loving others.

But it is also intriguing to think about the nuances of anger in the context of Christian faith. A close reading of the biblical references to anger reveals that, at times, anger is portrayed as a legitimate emotion and that to be able to *regulate* the emotion is something that can lead to a satisfactory outcome. That is, what psychological science tells us about the benefits of emotion regulation for mental health is corroborated by the Bible, in its wisdom.[11] For instance, it is striking to read passages that speak to the importance of being slow to anger (Prov. 14:29; James 1:19); anger, while legitimate, can be regulated in some form for the benefit of the self and others. Similarly, some passages warn against being quick to anger (e.g., Prov. 14:17) or being "given to anger" (Prov. 22:24–25 ESV). Ephesians 4:26 grants that we can "be angry" but tells us that in our anger, we must "not sin" and "not let the sun go down on [our] anger" (ESV). There is a clear directive not to let anger consume us, whether in duration or in the behaviors that follow it.

11. Marroquín et al., "Coping, Emotion Regulation, and Well-Being," 255–58.

Notably, God himself is described as being slow to anger in various instances, suggesting that a healthy regulating of one's emotion is what it means to image God in our everyday lives. Psalm 103:8 says, "The LORD is compassionate and gracious, *slow to anger*, abounding in love" (italics added). What is also noticeable is that many times when the "slow to anger" aspect of God is revealed in the Bible, it is accompanied by a statement that contrasts anger with other attributes. For instance, phrases like "compassionate and gracious" and "abounding in love" come up multiple times (Exod. 34:6; Neh. 9:17; Jon. 4:2). As such, one might perceive that anger's contrasting emotions or behaviors are compassion, grace, and steadfast love.

But as God himself demonstrates, the command to be slow in one's expression of anger is not a call to ignore indignities or injustices. Numbers 14:18 declares, "The LORD is slow to anger, abounding in love and forgiving sin and rebellion. Yet he does not leave the guilty unpunished; he punishes the children for the sin of the parents to the third and fourth generation." And many people in Christian communities will recognize the righteous anger that Jesus displayed when he drove out the merchants at the temple (Matt. 21:12).

An important question, then, is what the role of righteous or justified anger is in Christian communities, especially when connected to themes of culture, justice, and diversity.

The murder of George Floyd by police officers in 2020 had an impact on America—and indeed, the world—in a way that such injustice had not before. The fact that the killing was on-screen for the world to see, combined with the uneasy energy of the global COVID-19 pandemic, led to widespread angry protests. Communal anger was the primary emotion experienced and displayed by Black folks and their allies.

In my personal network of Christian folks, there was a mixed response to the anger displayed by the protesters. Those who criticized the anger tended to express sentiments to the effect of "What happened was unjust, but it also displeases God to respond with such strong emotions." Some went so far as to criticize the anger as sinful, and I would argue that in doing so, they lost sight of the injustice that started it all in the first place.

In contrast, public theologian Esau McCaulley writes that the intense individual and communal anger among Black folks should be understood in light of the racial oppression of the past and present.[12] Furthermore, he argues that the anger should be understood against the backdrop of God's response to our intense anger, which "is to enter that suffering alongside us as a friend and a redeemer."[13]

Another cultural example of how we in the Christian community can understand the role of collective anger comes from South Korea, my culture of origin. As I shared earlier in the book, I often lead a study-abroad program to South Korea. One of the cultural constructs that my American students engage in almost right away is the notion of *han*. Although it does not have an exact English equivalent, han can be understood as the Korean people's collective anger about historical injustices.[14] The historical trauma of the Korean people includes the Japanese colonial period and the Korean War; the latter split the Korean peninsula into northern and southern parts. My students feel a bit of the han—the internalized anger of South Koreans—whenever they learn about the atrocities of the Japanese colonial period and the continued absurdity and pain of one people group (i.e., North and South Koreans) still at war with themselves. These wounds of Korea are certainly han; they can also be described as manifestations of collective anger. Fully recognizing the validity of the collective anger, unequivocally affirming the suffering, is made possible when God's response of walking with us "as a friend and a redeemer" is realized.[15]

12. McCaulley, *Reading While Black*, 118–29.

13. McCaulley, *Reading While Black*, 130.

14. S. Kim, "Korean 'Han,'" 254; for more on han, see P. Kim, "Korean Constructs"; also see P. Kim, "Redeeming Korean Constructs," 11:17.

15. McCaulley, *Reading While Black*, 130.

Culture, Christian Faith, and Shame

In clinical and counseling psychology, shame is often considered evidence of psychological distress.[16] In interdependent cultures, however, shame can also be understood as an other-focused emotion; in their writing about other-focused emotion, Markus and Kitayama note that an other-focused emotion like shame "facilitates the reciprocal exchanges of well-intended actions, leads to further cooperative social behavior, and thus provides a significant form of self-validation for interdependent selves."[17] In other words, shame allows individuals to do their part in the culturally expected give-and-take in interpersonal situations, which allows them to maintain a desirable level of social standing.

An idea closely related to shame is the concept of face, and the preoccupation with losing face. Zane and Yeh define "social face" as a "person's set of socially-sanctioned claims concerning one's social character and social integrity in which this set of claims or this 'line' is largely defined by certain prescribed roles that one carries out as a member and representative of a group."[18] Simply put, then, the fear of losing face is the anxiety around losing one's social status or doing something to cause someone else to lose social status.

When I was teaching at a university in South Korea, I held office hours as I would back in the US. I was taken aback when a student brought cookies to my office hours, which is certainly not something that is expected in the US. When the next student brought a drink, I was perplexed enough to ask a colleague about this behavior. My colleague responded, "Students are doing their part to honor you. Not bringing the small 'gift' would make them feel like they are disrespecting you and, as a result, bringing shame to you and, ultimately, to themselves." Although the ethics of such

16. For examples of studies conceptualizing shame as evidence of pathology, see Gambin and Sharp, "Relations Between Empathy, Guilt, Shame and Depression," 381–83; Gilbert, "Relationship of Shame," 174–76.

17. Markus and Kitayama, "Culture and the Self," 235.

18. Zane and Yeh, "Use of Culturally-Based Variables," 126.

a practice are beyond the scope of this chapter, this story illustrates that shame is a critical ingredient in social interactions. Shame as an other-focused emotion was doing its part in triggering a behavior (i.e., gift giving) that strengthened and maintained an important relationship.

How must we make sense of shame from a Christian perspective? On the one hand, in light of having the debilitating shame of our sins lifted by Jesus, we can readily recognize shame as an emotion that goes counter to the recognition of our full worth before God. While not negating this dimension of shame, we must also consider its nuanced aspects, which emphasize a focus on others—a type of shame that spurs the lifting up of others and the trusting that others will do the same for us. If face concerns can serve as motivators for honoring people who deserve it, I think these concerns have a proper place in faithful Christian living.

Let's consider some biblical exhortations. Romans 12:10 encourages believers, "Love one another with brotherly affection. *Outdo one another in showing honor*" (ESV, italics added).[19] In other words, be really good—better than the other person—in showing honor. Likewise, in no uncertain terms, 1 Peter 2:17 calls for believers to "honor everyone" (ESV). Furthermore, it is not surprising to see God characterized as someone who seeks and deserves honor. In equating himself to God the Father, Jesus declares in John 5:23, "That all may honor the Son, just as they honor the Father. Whoever does not honor the Son does not honor the Father who sent him" (ESV). Moreover, God promises, "Those who honor me I will honor, but those who despise me will be disdained" (1 Sam. 2:30); this sounds a lot like the reciprocal element of face concerns in interdependent settings.

19. The idea of reciprocating honor is best captured in the ESV translation.

Key Takeaways

1. Some emotions are generalizable across cultures. The expression or suppression of emotions might differ depending on the cultural context.
2. Ego-focused emotions tend to be focused on advancing the goals of the self.
3. Other-focused emotions are focused on advancing the goals of the group.
4. Anger is a particular ego-focused emotion that can be understood in light of many aspects of Christianity.
5. Han and shame are other-focused emotions that can also be understood and critiqued from a Christian faith perspective.

Activities and Discussion Questions

1. What are some cultural and religious influences on how you view emotions? Do you think these influences are healthy or unhealthy?
2. This chapter mainly dealt with anger as an example of an emotion that is often brought up in the Bible. What are some other emotions that the Bible deals with? How is psychological science compatible with how the Bible talks about these particular emotions?
3. Find a research article that examines themes related to emotion, culture, and Christian faith. You might turn to journals like *Journal of Psychology and Theology*, *Journal of Psychology and Christianity*, or *Mental Health, Religion, and Culture* as starting points. Summarize the key findings. What are the strengths of the study? Any shortcomings? How do the findings inform everyday living, especially for those who are in the faith community?

4. Watch *The Color of Fear* (1994) by director Lee Mun Wah. (Warning: This is a heavy film, with explicit language.) Pay attention to parts where the characters express anger. What is your gut reaction to the anger? What might your reaction say about how you have been socialized? How might the anger expressed in the film be capturing the cultural differences that exist among the men in the room?

Case Study

Janette is a twenty-five-year-old Asian American college student. One day her roommate, Shana, discovers Janette in emotional distress and asks what is bothering her. Janette replies, "My parents just told me to come home for the weekend so that I can attend a family friend's wedding. But I do not want to go." In a puzzled tone, Shana says, "If that's the case, why can't you tell your parents the truth—that you do not wish to go?" Janette responds, "I wish I could. But it will bring shame to my parents if I skip out on this wedding."

1. How does this case study illustrate the pros and cons of other-focused emotions like shame?
2. List some phrases and words that come to mind when you think about Janette's posture toward her parents (e.g., "responsibility"). Next, think about how what you have jotted down might connect to the idea of interpersonal shame. Can you see a connection between interconnectedness and shame as a motivating emotion?
3. If you were Janette's Christian mentor (e.g., college pastor), what might you say to Janette about this situation? That is, how might a conversation about things like shame and honor be integrated into a conversation about faithful Christian living in Janette's circumstance?

8

Uncomfortable but Necessary

Grappling with Modern-Day Racism

Amy is a nineteen-year-old biracial Chinese American minoring in psychology at a small Christian institution in the Midwest US. During a group project discussion, a fellow student asked her, unprompted, "What are you?" Amy was bothered by this question, especially because it was a question that she readily recognized as referring to her mixed-race identity. Trying to keep her rising emotions in check, Amy calmly told the student that she found the question offensive, and she also briefly explained why it was insulting to biracial and multiracial folks (e.g., the dehumanization of mixed-race identities). After a few moments of uncomfortable silence, the same student said, "Why do you have to be so sensitive? I didn't mean anything by it." Amy felt even more frustrated and decided to approach her professor about the exchange. She requested to be switched to a different team for the group project. The professor responded by emphasizing the importance of Christian love and harmony, saying that being so angry about a trivial comment was not contributing to a grace-filled community.

Prejudice, Stereotype, Discrimination, and Racism

In everyday language, people sometimes use the terms "prejudice," "stereotype," "discrimination," and "racism" rather loosely, as if they were interchangeable ideas. But precise definitions are important for conceptualization and assessment of psychological constructs. Let's briefly review the key distinctions between these ideas. Prejudice is a disapproving evaluation of another person based on their group membership.[1] It is an internal dimension of relating to others who are different. For example, a study found that prejudice—that is, negative attitudes—against international students in the US was higher among certain American students (e.g., those who supported President Trump) and lower among others (e.g., those with a sense of university identity).[2] Stereotyping is also internal, but it refers to a generalization or categorization of other groups.[3] Unlike prejudice, which is always negative in content—you can't be positively prejudiced against someone—stereotypes can be favorable or negative. Can you think of an example of a positive racial stereotype?

It should be noted, however, that even though a stereotype may be positive in content, it may not be positive in impact. During the Democratic debate in 2019, presidential candidate Andrew Yang, an Asian American, quipped during one of his responses, "Now, I am Asian, so I know a lot of doctors."[4] Many people decried this joke as potentially dangerous in its perpetuation of generalizations about Asian Americans.[5] Furthermore, studies have shown that the model minority stereotype—the belief that all Asian Americans are exceptional in their achievement due to their hard work—is mixed in its outcome, especially if the stereotype is internalized by those who are stereotyped.[6]

1. Stangor, "Study of Stereotyping," 2.
2. Quinton, "Unwelcome on Campus?," 162.
3. Stangor, "Study of Stereotyping," 2–4.
4. Fix Team, "Transcript."
5. A. Wang, "Downside of Andrew Yang's Jokes."
6. Yoo et al., "Preliminary Report," 118–22.

Discrimination is the biased treatment of another person based on their group identity.[7] It is external or behavioral, so it is something that can be observed. For example, if a Black American teenager is followed around in a store because of their racial identity, we can argue that the act is infringing on the dignity and freedom of the teenager, and we can describe that behavior as a racially discriminatory act. Discrimination is what the typical American likely thinks of when they hear the word "racism." Later in this chapter, we will discuss racial microaggressions as contemporary forms of racial discrimination. Finally, "racism" refers to a power structure that is set up in a way that benefits one group over another.[8] Take a quick look at the leadership structure at a local college or university. What is racial representation like in the administration team, the group of people who hold the most power in the organization? If there is a skew toward a particular race, I would argue that racism is manifesting at the systemic or structural level.

Pause to Reflect

Using your own words and examples, define "prejudice," "stereotype," "discrimination," and "racism." Which terms are easier for you to define? More difficult to explain? Why might this be?

Racial Microaggressions

Have you heard of racial microaggressions? When I first started my teaching career, I would ask this question to my students, and only a few would raise their hands in response. But now if I were to ask this question, the majority of my students would say yes. Indeed, as a modern-day form of racial discrimination, microaggressions have garnered much interest among researchers

7. Neville and Pieterse, "Racism, White Supremacy, and Resistance," 163–65.
8. Tatum, "*Why Are All the Black Kids Sitting Together*," 89–97.

and clinicians alike. Prominent counseling psychologist Derald Wing Sue and his coauthors define "racial microaggressions" as follows: "Brief and commonplace daily verbal, behavioral, or environmental indignities, whether intentional or unintentional, that communicate hostile, derogatory, or negative racial slights and insults toward people of color."[9]

Let's unpack the definition a bit, because there is a lot packed into it. First, notice the "intentional or unintentional" phrase. That is, microaggressive acts can certainly be delivered on purpose, intending to harm the recipient, but microaggressions might also be done without a malicious intent, and perhaps even out of good intent. You might have heard the saying "Intent does not equal impact" to make the argument that psychological injury can occur regardless of whether a microaggressor intended harm.

Sports analysts sometimes (in my opinion) overanalyze injuries to star players by asking the unanswerable question: "Was the play that resulted in the injury a dirty play?" That is, they try to debate whether the player who injured another player meant to injure them. But regardless of what the truth might be, the outcome is the same: There is a hurt player, and their injury is independent of whether the play that caused it was intentional or unintentional. The same with the impact of racial microaggressions: The resulting psychological injury is valid, regardless of the intent of the perpetrator. Put differently, to argue that someone who feels invalidated or insulted should be gracious to a perpetrator of a microaggression is akin to telling an athlete who is injured that their injury is less valid because the other player did not mean harm.

The second aspect of this definition that I would like to highlight is that it describes microaggressions as "brief." During the COVID-19 pandemic, when anti-Asian racism was especially at the forefront of my mind, more than once while out in public I noticed disapproving or suspicious glances from strangers. Now there is no way for me to know with certainty that these folks

9. D. Sue et al., "Racial Microaggressions in Everyday Life," 271.

were looking at me due to anti-Asian sentiments, but given the context (the prevalent scapegoating of Asians for the coronavirus), I couldn't help but feel self-conscious and uncomfortable in my own land.

Going deeper, that microaggressions are brief also means that the recipient of the racial microaggression is often left to deal with the aftermath of everything—to pick up the pieces. Indeed, a fleeting microaggression can result in a moment of emotional and cognitive freeze, perhaps due to the shock of what has been said, and once the recipient of the microaggression has come to their senses, the interaction might be long finished, with no opportunity for justice or restoration. I would argue that this is precisely the reason that an intentional circling back to the microaggressive encounter, initiated by the microaggressor, can be a humble and powerful act. I once had a colleague who unintentionally said something to me about my racial identity that was microaggressive. But this friend emailed me later—they did not need to do so—to apologize for the brief interaction. To me, that simple gesture was a powerful example of how we as a loving Christian community can practice radical humility and intentional care for one another, by taking that extra step of circling back to the microaggression.

Finally, microaggressions are described as "daily" occurrences. Perhaps another good descriptor would be "frequent" or "more than once." That is, it is relatively easy to dismiss a single act of microaggression, but the harmful impact of racial discrimination is its reoccurrence for those who are in marginalized communities. Some have referred to the cumulative impact of microaggressions as "a thousand cuts."[10]

So, to sum up, microaggressions hurt regardless of intent, they are often brief encounters, and they are cumulative in their impact.

What might microaggressions confined to the Christian setting look like? To answer that question, I would like to first reflect on a Christian understanding of race and racism.

10. H. Yoon, "How to Respond."

Racism in Christian Contexts

The life that Christians are called to when it comes to racial relations is clear. Revelation 7:9–10 paints a glorious picture of a fully realized family of God: "After this I looked, and there before me was a great multitude that no one could count, from every nation, tribe, people and language, standing before the throne and before the Lamb. They were wearing white robes and were holding palm branches in their hands. And they cried out in a loud voice: 'Salvation belongs to our God, who sits on the throne, and to the Lamb.'"

Other New Testament passages also recognize the importance of unity in diversity: "There is neither Jew nor Gentile, neither slave nor free, nor is there male and female, for you are all one in Christ Jesus" (Gal. 3:28). Similarly, "Here there is no Gentile or Jew, circumcised or uncircumcised, barbarian, Scythian, slave or free, but Christ is all, and is in all" (Col. 3:11).

But faithful Christian living entails not only a recognition and celebration of diversity but also a meaningful embrace of the difficult but necessary conversations and emotions around racial relations. We need to begin with the fundamental truth that we are all created to reflect God's image (Gen. 1:27), and therefore the sin of racism violates this truth by degrading certain individuals and communities. As such, racism is deplorable in God's eyes. Veola Vazquez, Joshua Knabb, Charles Lee-Johnson, and Krystal Hays put it simply: "Sin is the root of all of humanity's problems in race relations, including racism and racial disunity. Racism itself is a sin and the result of sin."[11]

Moreover, the Bible provides directions for how we are to seek racial justice. A posture that we are commanded to take when it comes to racial relations is *empathy*—listening well to others. For instance, 1 Corinthians 12:26 notes that "if one part suffers, every part suffers with it; if one part is honored, every part rejoices

11. Vazquez et al., *Healing Conversations*, 18.

with it." Translated to the topic of racism and how it affects communities of color, when racial pain afflicts one community, others in Christian communities must practice empathy and find ways to grieve with that community. Indeed, the idea that we must weep and grieve with those most affected is a powerful truth that we must live into as believers. Fundamentally, this posture demonstrates that God is "close to the brokenhearted and saves those who are crushed in spirit" (Ps. 34:18). And racism can crush the spirit and break hearts.

In the graduation speech "You Need Two Eyes," Christian philosopher Nicholas Wolterstorff tells Calvin College graduates that in addition to the "eye" of knowledge or critical engagement, a second "eye," characterized by a posture of attunement to the hurting world and its people, is needed to help bring about shalom in God's world:

> It's with the second eye that the pain of the world and the hope for a new day enters your heart. "Blessed are those who mourn," said Jesus. He was not blessing those who go around moping. He was blessing those who discern all the ways in which life in this world falls short of justice and shalom, who then go on to say "This must not be," and who struggle to change things when they see the chance of doing so. The mourners are discontented visionaries. They will be comforted, says Jesus.[12]

And then there is the clear calling for Christians "to act justly and to love mercy and to walk humbly" with God (Mic. 6:8); the pursuit of justice is central to God's heart. That's a succinct overview of "the way things ought to be" for Christian communities and individuals when it comes to racial relations.

But sometimes, "the way things are" can reflect our individual and collective sins. There is a wealth of theoretical and empirical evidence, across academic disciplines, suggesting that Christian communities can sometimes perpetuate racist beliefs and actions.

12. Wolterstorff, "You Need Two Eyes."

In his bestselling book *The Color of Compromise*, Jemar Tisby provides compelling historical evidence of how the Christian church not only stayed silent in the face of racial injustice but sometimes was the leading entity in perpetuating racial violence against Black folks. As we already discussed in chapters 1 and 6, sociologists Michael Emerson and Christian Smith have provided empirical data demonstrating that the White evangelical community in the US tends to hold an incomplete understanding of racism—namely, that it is only about what one person does to another person, or that it is interpersonal in nature—thereby dismissing or minimizing its systemic or structural aspects.[13]

My own research team set out to study what modern racism, or racial microaggressions, might look like in a familiar Christian setting: Christian college campuses. Are there microaggressive messages or behaviors that are unique to Christian campuses? With a sample of three hundred students of color enrolled in Christian colleges, we eventually created a survey to ask about the microaggressions that were embedded in a Christian context. We found two key themes or factors. The first was the misapplication of theology or Christian beliefs in a way that was oppressive to students of color (e.g., students of color being told that they can overcome systemic racism if they simply follow the law). A second theme that emerged was the tendency to criticize students of color or their communities for various ways that racial discrimination or structural racism might manifest (e.g., students of color being criticized for depicting Christianity in non-White terms).[14] To reiterate, a commonality underlying these behaviors or messages is the weaponization of Christianity in a way that can lead to further psychological injury. Think back to the vignette at the beginning of this chapter. The professor's response to Amy can be described as an invalidation of her racialized experience—specifically, an

13. Emerson and Smith, *Divided by Faith*.

14. See P. Kim et al., "Racial Microaggressions on Christian Campuses" for measure items.

invalidation that is based on the idea that harmony should be pursued at all costs, even if it means that someone like Amy has to suffer.

Do the microaggression themes that I described here resonate with your experiences? Are there experiences that might not be captured within these themes?

Pause to Reflect

Recall a time when someone might have said or done something that sent a hurtful message regarding one or more of your social identities:

1. What did they say or do?
2. How did you feel after the interaction?
3. What hurtful underlying messages were conveyed?
4. Were there any implicit or explicit "Christian" messages underlying what was said or done?

But How Do We Heal?

Because of psychology's descriptive focus, much of the literature on race-related stress and trauma tends to focus on describing what these social stressors look like and how they might affect socioemotional outcomes. In my own research, I have repeatedly demonstrated the empirical association between the experience of racism and unfavorable psychological outcomes among students of color.[15]

But of course, another essential question to tackle in antiracism efforts would be what we can do in response to racism. For example, how do we go about responding to racial microaggressions in a way that is healing and constructive?

15. See P. Kim, "Religious Support Mediates the Racial Microaggressions," 151–52; P. Kim et al., "Racial Microaggressions, Cultural Mistrust," 667–67; P. Kim, "Revisiting and Extending the Role," 172–77.

In response to this need for an organized framework to understand effective responses to microaggressions, Dr. Derald Wing Sue and his coauthors propose that a response to microaggressions is complicated by some factors. For example, whom are we talking about? Is it the perpetuator, recipient, or a witness to a microaggression? Depending on the role of the person, the response will obviously change. And what is the goal in the situation? Is it, for example, to hold the person accountable? Is it to protect oneself from harm? Is it to educate?[16] Again, depending on your relational goal, your responses might differ.

There is also literature that speaks to the importance of forgiveness in response to experiences of racism. For example, in a sample of African American adults, the empirical relation between experiences of racial discrimination and depressive symptoms was weaker for those with a tendency to forgive.[17] Similarly, more hesitation to grant forgiveness for racial discrimination was associated with more vulnerability to depressive symptoms among African American men.[18] To be clear, the forgiveness emphasized in this literature is not premature forgiveness or the type that is imposed by those in power on those who have been wronged. Rather, the forgiveness is a psychological tool employed by a person as a coping strategy. When seen in that light, psychological science seems to confirm the importance of the forgiveness that the Christian tradition also emphasizes.

Beyond forgiveness, the literature reveals various forms of religious coping that might be utilized in response to racism. In chapters 1 and 6 I wrote about religious coping, further bifurcated as *positive* religious coping, which is a secure connection to God or what is considered sacred, and *negative* religious coping, which is a struggle with one's faith.[19] Experiencing racism was related

16. D. Sue et al., "Disarming Racial Microaggressions."

17. Brooks et al., "Moderating Effect of Dispositional Forgiveness," 515–16.

18. Powell et al., "Buried Hatchets," 653–54.

19. Pargament, *Psychology of Religion*, 1–20; Pargament et al., "Brief RCOPE," 54–55.

to negative religious coping, which in turn predicted psychological distress in a sample of Black Americans.[20] Interestingly, my own research has found that negative religious coping for Asian American Christians is actually protective against the deleterious impact of racism on mental health, suggesting that what is considered "negative" in negative religious coping might have context-dependent aspects.[21]

Within religious coping, support is a particular ingredient that seems promising as a protective factor. Veola Vazquez, Jaimee Stutz-Johnson, and Roy Sorbel found that religious support, when combined with less compartmentalization of identity (i.e., separating identities for multicultural individuals), was protective in the face of racial discrimination among biracial Black-White Christians.[22] During the COVID-19 pandemic, when churches were closed due to health regulations, an unintended but real consequence was that a critical source of support—the church and its people—for Black Americans was absent, resulting in a detriment of mental health among Black Americans.[23] The literature demonstrating the critical importance of the church community is yet another reminder that we need one another in moments and seasons of distress. Remember the biblical references I mentioned earlier that speak to the importance of others' responses to those who are afflicted? Psychological science supports this call by demonstrating the role of religious support and related variables for those who experience racial discrimination. The importance of relationships and communal support is especially heightened because racial discrimination can trigger one to turn less to church support, leading to more deleterious mental health outcomes.[24] More intentional support is needed to counter this tendency to turn away from effective social support whenever one experiences racial distress.

20. Szymanski and Obiri, "Religious Coping Styles," 451–54.
21. P. Kim et al., "Religious Coping Moderates the Relation," 90–91.
22. Vazquez et al., "Black-White Biracial Christians," 11–12.
23. DeSouza et al., "Coping with Racism."
24. P. Kim, "Religious Support Mediates the Racial Microaggressions," 151–52.

Christian psychologists Veola Vazquez, Joshua Knabb, Charles Lee-Johnson, and Krystal Hays articulate and expand on a framework for understanding and healing from racism with an apropos acronym: HEAL. This acronym stands for *humility* when interacting with one another around the topic of race and racialized experiences,[25] *empathy* for the experiences of the other person,[26] *acceptance* of the other person and their emotions,[27] and *love* that can be fully experienced only through an understanding of the love of God.[28] These four components that are so critical for faithful Christian living are also the ingredients for true healing in the aftermath of racism.

In my own reflections, I have especially resonated with the idea that Christlike humility is a virtue that offers much promise in restoring racial relations. Not just in racial relations but in cross-cultural relations in general, humility is a fundamental value that can aid people in connecting with and loving other folks, whether friends or strangers. Humility includes both internal (a reasonable view of oneself) and external (not elevating oneself above others) dimensions.[29] Humility in racial relations, then, requires the recognition of the fundamental truth of the internal dimension: I am a child of God who deserves to be treated with respect and, of course, this truth is also applicable to others. When that is violated by others or me, I must seek justice. At the same time, humility says that externally, I am not better than others in my sinful state; a truly humbling example of this is when I unintentionally find myself as a microaggressor.

In a *Christian Scholar's Review* blog, I wrote, "It's truly difficult to do so, but I sometimes share my own experiences of perpetuating microaggressions against others (including my own students!), and how I went about attempting to restore injured

25. Vazquez et al., *Healing Conversations*, 37–70.
26. Vazquez et al., *Healing Conversations*, 71–99.
27. Vazquez et al., *Healing Conversations*, 100–132.
28. Vazquez et al., *Healing Conversations*, 133–66.
29. Davis et al., "Relational Humility," 225.

relationships. These collective efforts stem from the practice of being appropriately vulnerable to my students, and going deeper, acknowledging the important truth that my fallenness is shared with the student who microaggressed against me (i.e., interpersonal aspect of humility)."[30]

In sum, from a Christian faith perspective, a multipronged understanding of healing from racism is necessary. We certainly benefit from individual interventions (e.g., intrapersonal religious coping, such as forgiveness). But also, psychological science and Christian perspectives resoundingly speak to the instrumentality of others (e.g., community) in healing from interpersonal and systemic wounds of racism. And in all these endeavors, Christlike humility is foundational for healing.

Pause to Reflect

Think of a microaggression that you have experienced.

1. What kind of a repair in the relationship was attempted, if there was one at all?
2. How did your relationship with the person shape the repairing of the relationship?
3. How might the principles outlined in this chapter shape future repair attempts?

Key Takeaways

1. Although related and sometimes used interchangeably in everyday language, the terms "prejudice," "stereotype," "discrimination," and "racism" mean different things in psychology. It is important that we use these terms accurately.

30. P. Kim, "When My Own Students Microaggress."

2. Racial microaggressions are contemporary forms of racial discrimination that psychologists are interested in studying and addressing.
3. Sometimes Christian communities perpetuate certain racial microaggressions with misapplied Christian beliefs.
4. Empathy is a helpful response to those who experience racial discrimination.
5. Healing from racial hurt is a complex process. Christian faith offers genuine hope for restoration of relationships and communities. Humility, in particular, is an important Christian virtue that can foster healing.

Activities and Discussion Questions

1. Go online and find examples (e.g., YouTube clips, social media posts) of prominent Christian figures responding well to the topic of racism. Also see if you can find examples of Christian leaders not responding well. Do you notice any common themes across these examples?
2. What are some stereotypes that you might have internalized about other groups? What do you think are the origins of these stereotypes?
3. Do you have any examples of when you were able to counter a stereotype about a cultural group you belong to?
4. What stereotypes have you internalized about your cultural groups?
5. Can you articulate why it is important to talk about racism from a Christian perspective?
6. How might Christian faith hurt those who are from marginalized communities?

Case Study

June is a Black woman who is a junior at a Christian liberal arts university in Texas. After the murder of George Floyd by police officers, June felt compelled to join the protests on and off campus. During a Bible study that she regularly attends, she shared about her experiences, including her motivation for protesting and the positive effects she experienced as a result of participating in communal racial justice efforts. After she shared, a few members spoke up about the importance of harmony and peace and how the protests went against Christian principles. One student even noted, "Why are we so angry all the time? We should just love one another." June felt angered and confused by the responses from this community, a community that she considered an important network.

1. Can you name the microaggression(s) exemplified in this scenario?
2. How might the member who made the hurtful comment benefit from a deeper understanding of anger as a collective emotion?
3. How might the group members have responded instead?
4. What might June do in response to the invalidations?
5. Why do you think it is so difficult for Christian communities to accept and validate the collective anger of others?
6. How can Christian communities cultivate a culture that laments and embraces others' experiences of pain instead of invalidating them?

9

Faith Shapes Beliefs, Expression, and Treatment

Mental Health

> You are . . . proof that Western therapy does not work on Eastern minds.
>
> —Danny to Amy, from the Netflix show *Beef*[1]

Which topic in psychology interests you the most? My guess is that most of you are interested in mental health. Many psychology students are drawn to psychology as a discipline, in part, because of their own experiences surrounding mental health. Furthermore, whether we realize it or not, how we think about mental health and its related ideas is profoundly shaped by culture. This chapter's opening quote, from the Netflix series *Beef*, succinctly captures how sometimes cultural differences can contribute to disparity in the helpfulness of professional counseling.

1. Lee Sung Jin, creator, *Beef*, season 1, episode 10, "Figures of Light," directed by Lee Sung Jin, aired April 6, 2023, https://www.netflix.com/title/81447461.

When psychologists discuss mental health, they tend to ask three different but related questions:

1. What are the causes of mental health distress? (causal or etiology beliefs)
2. What does mental health distress look like? (features or symptoms)
3. How can the distress be reduced or eliminated? (treatment)

Culture shapes the answers to each question. In this chapter, I will unpack the answers, at times engaging them from a faith perspective.

Causal or Etiology Beliefs

Regardless of cultural background, people tend to recognize that causes of mental illness are complicated and multifaceted. But certain explanations of mental illness show up again and again across cultures. In a study aimed at creating and validating a survey of etiology beliefs, Brandon Knettel surveyed international students in the US, and the following etiology beliefs emerged (factors that are reflected in the Mental Illness Attribution Questionnaire): supernatural influences, interpersonal/stress factors, way of living, physical health–related reasons, substance-related factors, individual shortcomings, and genetic/biological reasons.[2]

Given the focus of this book, let's take a few moments to zoom in on the *supernatural* influences. Do you feel that mental illnesses can be caused by factors such as lack of faith, God's punishment, a sinful heart, and so on? I grew up in a Christian context that emphasized a well-intentioned but inaccurate spiritual understanding of mental illness. For example, a pervasive message was that through fervent prayer, any mental health distress could be

2. Knettel, "Attribution Through the Layperson's Lens," 35, 42; for details on how the attribution factors emerged, see pp. 34–39.

overcome. For those suffering from mental health distress, the implication was that they were not praying hard enough. I quickly unlearned some of these inaccuracies as I immersed myself in the field of psychology, but some of the spiritual etiology beliefs still linger in their impact. As such, the major cultural influences on my causal beliefs are my Korean culture, Korean Christian culture, mainstream American culture, and the world of psychology that I have been socialized into.

Pause to Reflect

Take a moment to reflect on your own understanding of spiritual influences on mental health. Especially reflect on the *cultural* influences on your perspectives regarding what causes mental illness, including which influences might be stronger.

My religious background as a Christian intersected with my Asian and Korean cultural contexts to shape my etiology beliefs. This story is consistent with what psychologists have found through empirical inquiries. Joana Salifu Yendork, Gladys Beryl Brew, Elizabeth A. Sarfo, and Lily Kpobi conducted a qualitative study with Ghanaians from neoprophetic churches.[3] They found that participants held diverse viewpoints about mental health that were not unlike the ones I mentioned earlier; both environmental and biological factors (some explanations combined the two) were endorsed by the participants. Notably, even the identification of drugs as a possible trigger for mental health was based on some cultural assumptions. Spiritual explanations included beliefs that mental illness might be a curse on the individuals and their family. Alternatively, mental illness was also viewed as a spiritual attack intentionally delivered from another person. Finally, the interactions of factors such as lifestyle and spirituality were also highlighted. For example, participants

3. Salifu Yendork et al., "Mental Illness Has Multiple Causes," 650–52.

noted that people who act in a way that goes against society are getting what they deserve if they are afflicted by mental illness. One participant gave the example of someone's marital infidelity as a cultural violation that can lead to the spiritual affliction of mental illness.[4]

Why am I highlighting the key findings of this study? After all, for many of us living and studying in the US context, the above findings are not as familiar. However, I contend that we rely on a mix of Christian and cultural perspectives in thinking about the causal factors underlying someone's mental health distress.

Features or Symptoms of Mental Illness

What do mental illnesses look like? And how does psychological distress express or suppress itself against the backdrop of culture? What is distinct about psychological distress is that, unlike something like COVID-19 (which I caught while living in Korea and then again in the US, with very similar symptoms), its features can depend on culture. That is, culture can encourage the expression of some mental health symptoms and discourage the expression of others. Consistent with this idea, a cross-cultural comparison of people who hear voices found that Indian and Ghanaian patients with schizophrenia reported more positive themes in their auditory hallucinations, whereas American patients with schizophrenia reported mostly negative themes.[5] Another common example in psychological sciences is regarding somatization, which is the "the expression of psychological disturbance in physical (bodily) symptoms."[6] A study comparing Malaysian Chinese and Australian Caucasians with depression found that the former group was more likely to experience depression through somatic symptoms,

4. Salifu Yendork et al., "Mental Illness Has Multiple Causes," 654–62.

5. Luhrmann et al., "Differences in Voice-Hearing," 42–43.

6. *APA Dictionary of Psychology*, "somatization," last updated April 19, 2018, https://dictionary.apa.org/somatization.

whereas the latter was more likely to endorse cognitive experiences underlying depression.[7]

Not only can there be a difference in intensity of expression of certain symptoms, but culture can also shape what is viewed as pathology in the first place. Did you know that there was a time when the desire to escape slavery by Black Americans was deemed a diagnosable illness? "Drapetomania" is the official name that Samuel A. Cartwright invented in 1851 to describe this.[8] As ridiculous and oppressive as this diagnosis sounds to us now, it illustrates that cultural norms can shape what we consider to be mental illness.

On the other hand, it is also important to recognize that many features of mental illnesses are shared across cultures. For instance, the World Health Organization consistently names depression as a disorder affecting people across the globe and lists factors such as suicide as clear, generalizable symptoms of depression.[9]

But how do we know when something (e.g., a behavior) should be considered pathological?

Pathology? Normal Behavior? How Can We Tell?

If I were to tell you that I occasionally talk to my deceased aunt, what would you think of me? What questions might you ask me to determine whether this is problematic (i.e., pathological)?

If you are familiar with a Western understanding of psychopathology, you might suspect that this is a hallucination or delusion. But is any kind of a break from reality psychopathological? Or are there cultural and other considerations that might give us pause?

Let's build on this scenario. Say a young woman named Trinity has mentioned talking to her dead grandmother and is relaying the words to her family. Trinity's grandmother passed away two

7. Parker et al., "Do the Chinese Somatize Depression?," 289–91.

8. Eakin, "Bigotry as Mental Illness."

9. "Depressive Disorder (Depression)," World Health Organization, March 31, 2023, https://www.who.int/news-room/fact-sheets/detail/depression.

and a half weeks ago. Her professor is concerned about her and has referred her to the counseling center.

Joseph Westermeyer proposes asking the following questions (i.e., heuristics) to determine whether a hallucination or delusion is problematic:[10]

1. *Are others in the community supportive of the behavior(s) in question, or are they unsupportive?* This criterion captures the importance of communal agreement on mental health and what should be considered psychopathology. That is, social norms determine whether a behavior should be considered pathology. For Trinity, it would be important to assess if her family and friends are worried about the conversations with the deceased grandmother or are instead accepting or even happy about them.

   In the movie *Lars and the Real Girl*, the protagonist (Lars, played by Ryan Gosling) develops a romantic relationship with a life-size doll. In a simultaneously moving and humorous part of the movie, Lars has the doll accompany him to a reading session at a local school, and he also brings her to a hairstylist for a haircut. In these scenes, the reactions of those interacting with Lars (and with his "girlfriend") demonstrate heartfelt communal support for Lars.[11] The point of these scenes is not to argue in favor of the "go along with it" approach as a long-term solution for delusions. Rather, the scenes provide a refreshing look into the power of communal support in response to commonly pathologized behavior.
2. *Does the behavior in question last long or for only a short period of time?* This criterion places some weight on the duration of the behavior in question. The longer the behavior lasts, the more likely it is that a clinician will lean toward a diagnosis. Conversely, the shorter the behavior lasts, the more

10. Westermeyer, "Cultural Factors," 473.
11. Craig Gillespie, dir., *Lars and the Real Girl* (Metro-Goldwyn-Mayer, 2007).

likely a clinician is to *not* diagnose the person. The logic is that someone who is in a state of significant psychological distress will have symptoms that persist, but someone who is not necessarily experiencing pathology will experience more transient symptoms.

In the case of Trinity, if the conversations with her grandmother were most intense in the days following her death but became less so in the weeks that followed, the behavior in question might not be indicative of psychopathology.

3. *After the person experiences the behavior in question, is the person doing things that are socially accepted and beneficial to the self? How about before the behavior in question?* This criterion is a pragmatic understanding of psychopathology. Take the example of self-harm; we can readily identify maladaptive antecedents to the behavior (e.g., feeling angry), as well as the outcomes of such a behavior (e.g., feelings of guilt).[12]

   For Trinity, then, it would be helpful to get an assessment of the circumstances that might have triggered the behavior in question, as well as how the behavior makes her feel and behave afterward. For example, are the conversations with her grandmother followed by good outcomes, such as being able to go to her classes, connecting with social networks, and so on? If so, we can reasonably surmise that the behavior in question might be an adaptive coping behavior.

4. *Does the behavior in question lead to a decrease in self-esteem and collective honor?* This criterion is similar to number 3 in that it is interested in the correlates or outcomes of the behavior in question. For instance, when clients report hearing voices that others do not hear and seeing things that others do not see, professional counselors are trained to ask about the specific contents of the auditory or visual

12. Chapman and Dixon-Gordon, "Emotional Antecedents and Consequences," 546–48.

messages. If a voice inside one's head is consistently critical of the self, it is reasonable to surmise that self-esteem will be deleteriously affected. Likewise, if the behavior in question is causing embarrassment and dishonor for the family and other close relationships, then this collective dishonor might mean that the behavior should be considered a pathology.

Therefore, for Trinity, it would be important to assess if her experience of communicating with her deceased grandmother is boosting or reducing individual and collective esteem.

5. *Are other psychological symptoms present?* That is, does the behavior in question come with any less ambiguous features of psychological distress, such as a co-occurring mood or anxiety symptoms? For Trinity, it would be helpful to ask about any other psychological symptoms that might be accompanying her experiences.
6. *If there are suspected hallucinations or delusions, do the hallucinations and delusions make sense in the cultural context?* I grew up in a Christian culture that accepted and even respected spiritual experiences such as speaking in tongues, seeing visions, and so on. For someone who is not familiar with this cultural context, however, witnessing another person having this kind of out-of-body experience can feel strange or even frightening. When I lead my South Korea study-abroad program, on a Sunday I take my American students to Yoido Full Gospel Church, one of the largest churches in the world.[13] Students, including my Christian students, are often startled when the thousands of people gathered at the church start praying out loud in unison. At the same time, they quickly understand that this type of chanting, while unfamiliar to them, is something that is part

13. "Largest Churches in the World 2025," *World Population Review*, accessed May 10, 2025, https://worldpopulationreview.com/country-rankings/largest-churches-in-the-world.

of the religious ritual in this Christian cultural setting. But if someone were to pray in the same manner while, say, utilizing public transportation, they would be perceived very differently.

One more example that is a bit silly: More than once I have mistakenly concluded that someone was talking to themselves, when in fact they were talking into a Bluetooth device. Context matters when determining whether a behavior is pathological. For Trinity, the context of grieving is important to keep in mind in understanding and diagnosing the behavior in question.

One Critique

A common thread running through Westermeyer's heuristics is the consideration of *context* in helping to determine whether a behavior should be deemed pathological. As such, there is a reliance on the response of others to gauge the normality of a behavior. That is, do other people also engage in the behavior (or at least support it)? Or is the behavior in question an aberration from the typical?

How should Christian communities grapple with such dependence on social norms?

On the one hand, from a Christian faith perspective, I believe that it *is* important to consider the norms of one's culture when determining what is healthy behavior. That is, in some sense, it is biblical to be sensitive to the needs and preferences of others and, if possible, to conform to those needs and preferences.

For example, Romans 14:19–21 exhorts believers in this way: "Let us therefore make every effort to do what leads to peace and to mutual edification. Do not destroy the work of God for the sake of food. All food is clean, but it is wrong for a person to eat anything that causes someone else to stumble. It is better not to eat meat or drink wine or to do anything else that will cause your brother or sister to fall." Notice how in this passage the apostle

Paul, speaking specifically to the behavior of eating certain kinds of food, is encouraging believers to conform to the needs and perspectives of others.

Similarly, 1 Corinthians 12 could be understood as a call to recognize the importance of conforming to the norms—the different parts of the body being attuned to one another (see v. 25)—for the sake of unity.

If conformity to norms is a good thing, then behaviors that go against community norms might be reasonably viewed as unhealthy. In that sense, Westermeyer's heuristics are compatible with a biblical understanding of individual and communal health.

On the other hand, there can be downsides to reliance on others' expectations and perceptions to assess what is healthy. From a Christian perspective, there are times when social norms should be violated for faithful Christian living. That is, what society or culture considers normative might not always be the best barometer for what is truly good. As Galatians 1:10 states, "Am I now trying to win the approval of human beings, or of God? Or am I trying to please people? If I were still trying to please people, I would not be a servant of Christ." This passage implies that faithfully seeking after God means that there might be times when pleasing other people by meeting their expectations is not possible.

As mentioned earlier, "drapetomania" was once a culturally normative diagnosis. This is an example of how societal norms (e.g., the acceptance of slavery) can directly influence the creation of an absurd diagnosis. The cultural context influenced its acceptance, but in retrospect, it should not have been accepted as a medical diagnosis.

Simply relying on what society accepts as pathology or nonpathology can lead us astray. Sometimes biblical principles call us to break away from what others might expect of us. Of course, to break societal norms requires courage, but it might actually be the healthy thing to do in certain situations.

Jesus turned many societal norms on their heads: He drove away the merchants at the temple (Matt. 21:12–13), and he connected with people of minoritized or despised groups, such as the Samaritan woman (John 4) and the tax collector Zacchaeus (Luke 19). It was rather radical for Jesus to interact with these individuals. That is, he went against cultural norms in making these meaningful connections. In refusing to conform to the norms, Jesus was exemplifying the notion that what is most noble—healthiest, to use the language we are using in this chapter—might be a deviation from cultural or social norms. It may be healthiest for us to take seriously the commandment "Do not conform to the pattern of this world" (Rom. 12:2).

So far, I have discussed cross-cultural differences in causal beliefs of mental illness. I have also reflected on expressions of mental illnesses, including when something should be considered a disorder. Let's now shift our focus to the third component—namely, how we respond to psychological distress.

Culture and Views of Treatment

It is important to recognize that cultural frameworks, such as how one thinks about the self, can profoundly shape the understanding of mental health treatment. As such, I appreciate the work of Laurence Kirmayer, who articulates how various forms of understanding the self can lead to the emphasis of certain cultural values, develop a locus of agency, form ways of telling stories about the self, and ultimately influence methods of healing.[14] Kirmayer writes, "If the concept of the person varies cross-culturally, then the goals and methods of therapeutic change must also differ."[15] Kirmayer uses the terms "egocentric," "sociocentric," "ecocentric," and "cosmocentric" to capture the different understandings of the self.[16]

Although Kirmayer is likely not writing specifically from a Christian faith vantage point, I can readily see how some of these

14. Kirmayer, "Psychotherapy and the Cultural Concept," 237–51.
15. Kirmayer, "Psychotherapy and the Cultural Concept," 233.
16. Kirmayer, "Psychotherapy and the Cultural Concept," 244.

definitions of the self can reinforce biblical perspectives about healing, whereas others might be critiqued from a Christian faith perspective.

Let me begin with the *egocentric* configuration of the self, a dominant perspective in Western conceptualization of mental health. Kirmayer refers to individualism as the "valorization of the self."[17] The Bible speaks of the value of *one* person before God. Whether it's the parable of the shepherd going after the one lost sheep even if it means leaving the ninety-nine (Luke 15:1–7), the reminder that "I am fearfully and wonderfully made" (Ps. 139:14), or God declaring, "Before I formed you in the womb I knew you, before you were born I set you apart; I appointed you as a prophet to the nations" (Jer. 1:5), it is clear that God sees the one person.

In the story of the Samaritan woman at the well (John 4), the woman has several "big picture" questions for Jesus (e.g., sociopolitical and gender-related inquiries, questions about where worship should take place, questions about spiritual water). But while Jesus does respond to these big questions, he also does not neglect the individual in front of him. In fact, he is laser focused on asking her about her private life (e.g., the fact that she has no husband and has lived with multiple men) and narrating back her individual story. In other words, Jesus truly sees her, including the parts of her life that are deeply private and individual. In my read of this passage, it seems like Jesus is conveying the message to the Samaritan woman that her individual story matters, and matters a great deal, for her well-being.

Some of the most popular modalities for individual psychotherapy emphasize an egocentric understanding of healing. Whether it is the ultra-individualistic person-centered approach of Carl Rogers,[18] the deep individual introspection required of psychodynamic approaches, or the mechanistic and linear emphasis of

17. Kirmayer, "Psychotherapy and the Cultural Concept," 241.
18. See Rogers, *Client-Centered Therapy*; Rogers, *On Becoming a Person*.

behavioral and cognitive therapies,[19] the well-known and widely practiced psychotherapies in the US context elevate the individual to the highest level.

In contrast to the egocentric emphasis, the *sociocentric* perception of the self and the resulting healing model argue that mental health interventions should be understood in light of relationships with other people.[20] In the Christian tradition, community is an important aspect of healthy living. Philippians 2:3 implores believers to "in humility value others" above themselves. Acts 2:44–45 narrates the epitome of faithful communal living: "The believers were together and had everything in common. They sold property and possessions to give to anyone who had need."

Moreover, the sociocentric perspective calls for multiple voices to speak into the problems of the individual. I am reminded of Job, who had multiple friends speaking into the possible reasons for his immense suffering and offering (what they thought was helpful) advice. They might not have been accurate in their attributions of Job's troubles, but their verbal input into Job's distress is an example of the emphasis on relationships and having someone speak into the problem.[21]

Popular professional counseling approaches in the Western context tend not to emphasize the perspectives of others as much. In the classic training film "Three Approaches to Psychotherapy" (1965), three psychologists (Carl Rogers, Fritz Perls, and Albert Ellis) engage in counseling with a woman named Gloria; the hyperindividualism that dominates Western modes of psychotherapy is perhaps most strongly exemplified in Carl Rogers's session. When Gloria discloses her struggle to balance her responsibilities to her daughter and her own desires for men, Rogers's repeated response is for Gloria to focus solely on her individual

19. See Tan, *Counseling and Psychotherapy*, for more on critiques of these major therapy modalities.
20. Kirmayer, "Psychotherapy and the Cultural Concept," 242.
21. Kirmayer, "Psychotherapy and the Cultural Concept," 244–45.

wants and needs.[22] Had Rogers embraced a more sociocentric understanding of the self, he might have encouraged Gloria to be more attuned to the voices of others who also are an important part of her identity.

Under the sociocentric perspective, the role of other people for healing also extends to attitudes toward and perceptions of counseling. When I worked at university counseling centers as a counselor, it was not uncommon for me to encounter students who were hesitant to see a professional counselor, not because they themselves were not convinced that therapy was helpful but because their family members (e.g., parents) were resistant to the notion of them meeting with a mental health professional. In these situations, I sometimes witnessed colleagues, supervisors, and myself minimizing or even dismissing the influence of others, in essence saying, "Well, *you* know that counseling is valuable. Just ignore your parents—they are trying to prevent you from receiving something that is beneficial for you." Even if this message was well intentioned, I can see how it reflected a cultural blind spot of those who practice professional counseling under an individualistic framework.

I coauthored a research study focused on the cultural and social influences on attitudes toward counseling among Asian American college students.[23] We found that the perception of how others feel about counseling (e.g., how my loved one views professional counseling) influenced a student's individual willingness to see a professional counselor. Notably, this sensitivity toward the beliefs of others was especially pronounced for those who had internalized more traditional cultural values reflecting respect for authority and attunement to others. A sociocentric view of counseling, when working with someone from an Asian American background, would then consider that there might be external forces acting as a barrier to professional counseling.

22. Everett L. Shostrom, dir., "Client-Centered Therapy," with Carl Rogers, part 1 of *Three Approaches to Psychotherapy* (Psychological Films, 1965).

23. P. Kim and Park, "Testing a Multiple Mediation Model," 298–99.

Now let's briefly consider the compatibility of the *ecocentric* (an emphasis on nature) and *cosmocentric* (a focus on the lasting influence of those who have passed) perspectives of healing from a Christian faith perspective.[24] Your gut reaction might be one of skepticism, or even outright rejection, to the possibility that an ecocentric or (especially) a cosmocentric perspective might have connecting points to your Christian faith.

At the same time, I believe that Christians should take some elements of the ecocentric and cosmocentric modes of healing seriously. The ecocentric understanding of the self, especially in its emphasis on balance and harmony for healing,[25] is an important consideration for faithful and responsible Christian living. Living harmoniously with one another is an important consideration for healing. Taking care of nature is an important Christian calling. And the pursuit of balance and harmony *within* oneself has important connections to Christian faith.

What about a cosmocentric perspective on healing? I am struck by Kirmayer's inclusion of ancestral focus in individual and collective healing.[26] A merit of the cosmocentric perspective is in its reminder that we can learn much from the experiences of others, including from those who lived before us, for the sake of our healing. The Bible refers to the faithful people who have come before us as "a great cloud of witnesses" (Heb. 12:1). And the remembrance of the past is not just about the good; in reference to a painful, collective event (e.g., a locust invasion), Joel 1:3 instructs the people not to forget: "Tell it to your children, and let your children tell it to their children, and their children to the next generation."

This theme of remembering for the sake of collective health is echoed in Esther 9:28. In this passage, there is a call to remember across generations, to recall God's deliverance and to celebrate it: "These days should be remembered and observed in every generation by every family, and in every province and in every city.

24. Kirmayer, "Psychotherapy and the Cultural Concept," 244–46.
25. Kirmayer, "Psychotherapy and the Cultural Concept," 244.
26. Kirmayer, "Psychotherapy and the Cultural Concept," 244.

And these days of Purim should never fail to be celebrated by the Jews—nor should the memory of these days die out among their descendants." Again, the implication is clear: Not forgetting across generations is a good thing for individual and collective health.

To conclude, holistic healing must be pursued as an intergenerational endeavor. In her memoir *Bipolar Faith: A Black Woman's Journey with Depression and Faith*, Monica Coleman writes the following powerful description of visiting an Africa-centered cultural art center:

> I danced ancient rhythms. I danced for the ancestors. I danced the harvest for Grandma and her siblings who picked cotton for low wages. I danced the harvest for Nana who taught me how to make biscuits and cakes. I danced the warrior for Grandaddy who tried to be strong for his family but didn't know how. I danced for my family ancestors. I danced with them.
>
> I was surprised by how much it felt like worship. I adopted the stories of the dance as my own. . . . I danced and prayed. I danced and thanked. I danced and celebrated. My body spoke in ways my voice could not: Thank you for the earth. Thank you for the harvest. Thank you for my sisters. Thank you for the ancestors. Thank you. Thank . . . God.[27]

Coleman's account, in particular her intentional connection to her ancestors as she worships God, is compatible with Kirmayer's cosmocentric perspective.

Key Takeaways

1. Culture and Christian faith interact to shape one's beliefs about the causes of psychological distress.

27. Coleman, *Bipolar Faith*, 214.

2. Expressions of certain symptoms, as well as what constitutes a symptom, might differ across cultures.
3. Methods of determining pathology should be critiqued from a Christian perspective. In particular, reliance on social norms can be compatible with Christian faith but can also provide some points of tension.
4. Responses to mental illness (i.e., counseling, healing methods) should also be evaluated in light of Christian faith.

Activities and Discussion Questions

1. Consider some of the major theoretical orientations (i.e., ways of doing professional counseling) in psychology, such as person-centered, psychodynamic, cognitive, and behavioral therapies. From a cultural perspective, such as one of the various construals of the self, what are the strengths and weaknesses of these approaches? What about from a Christian faith perspective?
2. What beliefs do you have about the causes of mental illness? How has your cultural background influenced this perspective? What about your religious background? How have your beliefs changed over time?
3. Choose a movie or a series that deals with themes of mental health, culture, and religion. *Beef* (the opening quote of this chapter is from this show) is a powerful example of such a show, but it is also not for everyone. After watching the movie or series, reflect on how culture, religion, and mental health were portrayed. Do you think the movie or show added to the stigma or helped to destigmatize mental illness? Do you think that what you watched was a realistic portrayal of how Christian communities tend to respond to mental health? Provide specific examples.

4. Choose a behavior that you are unsure about—something that might or might not be considered psychopathology. Perhaps you see it within yourself, or you might have observed a loved one, an acquaintance, or a classmate engaging in this behavior. Apply Westermeyer's heuristics to help you reflect on whether this behavior should be considered psychopathology.

Case Study

Edgar is a twenty-three-year-old Filipino American college student. His political science professor walked him over to the university counseling center, telling the intake counselor that he was worried that Edgar was showing signs of depression. On the referral form, the professor made several observations about Edgar, such as a lack of verbal participation in class, dozing off during lectures, and frequent absences or tardiness. When alone with the intake counselor, Edgar told her, "I only came to the counseling center because I wanted to honor my professor. I don't think I need psychological help." When asked why he thinks he does not need professional counseling, Edgar explained that he regularly talks to his church pastor about the difficult things in his life. "I trust my pastor completely, because he is ordained by God to do good works," Edgar declared. Edgar also added, "My parents would be so angry if they found out that I am talking to a professional counselor. They would be so ashamed." When pressed, Edgar admitted to the counselor that he does experience some sadness "here and there," unexplained bodily symptoms like headaches and stomach pains, and intense loneliness at times. He also has difficulty sleeping and eating like he used to. But he reiterated to the counselor that he does not feel like professional counseling can help him, stating, "No offense. I don't trust therapists. It goes against my religion."

Imagine that you are Edgar's intake counselor and answer the following questions:

1. How might you try to assist Edgar in gaining a helpful understanding of what professional counseling is?
2. What is a helpful way to explain to someone like Edgar about mental health and counseling from a Christian perspective? What is an unhelpful way?
3. How might you validate the distrust of counseling (especially if it is due to cultural reasons) and, at the same time, work to decrease the distrust?
4. What kind of questions might you ask to assess if what Edgar is reporting might be pathology?
5. What are the pros and cons of relying on clergy members (e.g., pastors) for mental health interventions?
6. If Edgar does end up utilizing your counseling services, how might you tailor your interventions to be most helpful to him? That is, what kind of cultural considerations will shape how you deliver your counseling services?

Bibliography

Abe-Kim, Jennifer, Sumie Okazaki, and Sharon G. Goto. "Unidimensional Versus Multidimensional Approaches to the Assessment of Acculturation for Asian American Populations." *Cultural Diversity and Ethnic Minority Psychology* 7, no. 3 (2001): 232–46. https://doi.org/10.1037/1099-9809.7.3.232.

Abraído-Lanza, Ana F., Adria N. Armbrister, Karen R. Flórez, and Alejandra N. Aguirre. "Toward a Theory-Driven Model of Acculturation in Public Health Research." *American Journal of Public Health* 96, no. 8 (2006): 1342–46. https://doi.org/10.2105/AJPH.2005.064980.

APA Task Force on Race and Ethnicity Guidelines in Psychology. "APA Guidelines on Race and Ethnicity in Psychology." American Psychological Association, August 2019. https://www.apa.org/about/policy/guidelines-race-ethnicity.pdf.

Arnett, Jeffrey J. "The Neglected 95%: Why American Psychology Needs to Become Less American." *American Psychologist* 63, no. 7 (2008): 602–14. https://doi.org/10.1037/0003-066X.63.7.602.

Atkinson, Donald R., George Morten, and Derald Wing Sue, eds. *Counseling American Minorities*. 5th ed. McGraw Hill, 1998.

Bang, Keeyeon, and Rodney K. Goodyear. "South Korean Supervisees' Experience of and Response to Negative Supervision Events." *Counselling Psychology Quarterly* 27, no. 4 (2014): 353–78. https://doi.org/10.1080/09515070.2014.940851.

Barker-Hackett, Lori. "African Americans in the New Millennium: A Continued Search for Our True Identity." In *Culturally Diverse Mental Health*, edited by Jeffery Scott Mio and Gayle Y. Iwamasa. Brunner-Routledge, 2013.

Berry, John W. "Lead Article: Immigration, Acculturation, and Adaptation." *Applied Psychology* 46, no. 1 (1997): 5–34. https://doi.org/10.1111/j.1464-0597.1997.tb01087.x.

Bertrand, Marianne, and Sendhil Mullainathan. "Are Emily and Greg More Employable than Lakisha and Jamal? A Field Experiment on Labor Market Discrimination." *American Economic Review* 94, no. 4 (2004): 991–1013. https://doi.org/10.1257/0002828042002561.

Betancourt, Hector, and Steven R. López. "The Study of Culture, Ethnicity, and Race in American Psychology." *American Psychologist* 48, no. 6 (1993): 629–37. https://doi.org/10.1037/0003-066X.48.6.629.

Bonhoeffer, Dietrich. *Life Together: The Classic Exploration of Christian Community*. HarperOne, 1954.

Bourhis, Richard Y., Léna Céline Moïse, Stéphane Perreault, and Sacha Senécal. "Towards an Interactive Acculturation Model: A Social Psychological Approach." *International Journal of Psychology* 32, no. 6 (1997): 369–86. https://doi.org/10.1080/002075997400629.

Bradley, Laura. "*Inside Out* Director Pete Docter Explains Why Pixar Remade Certain Scenes for Foreign Viewers," *Slate*, July 30, 2015, https://slate.com/culture/2015/07/inside-out-director-pete-docter-explains-why-pixar-re-animated-certain-scenes-like-the-broccoli-scene-for-international-audiences.html.

Brislin, Richard W. "Back-Translation for Cross-Cultural Research." *Journal of Cross-Cultural Psychology* 1, no. 3 (1970): 185–216. https://doi.org/10.1177/135910457000100301.

Broesch, Tanya, Alyssa N. Crittenden, Bret A. Beheim et al. "Navigating Cross-Cultural Research: Methodological and Ethical Considerations." *Proceedings of the Royal Society B: Biological Sciences* 287, no. 1935 (2020). https://doi.org/10.1098/rspb.2020.1245.

Brooks, Jasmin R., Judy H. Hong, Ijeoma J. Madubata, Mary O. Odafe, Soumia Cheref, and Rheeda L. Walker. "The Moderating Effect of Dispositional Forgiveness on Perceived Racial Discrimination and Depression for African American Adults." *Cultural Diversity and Ethnic Minority Psychology* 27, no. 3 (2021): 511–20. https://doi.org/10.1037/cdp0000385.

Captari, Laura E., Laura Shannonhouse, Joshua N. Hook et al. "Prejudicial and Welcoming Attitudes Toward Syrian Refugees: The Roles of Cultural Humility and Moral Foundations." *Journal of Psychology and Theology* 47, no. 2 (2019): 123–39. https://doi.org/10.1177/0091647119837013.

Chapman, Alexander L., and Katherine L. Dixon-Gordon. "Emotional Antecedents and Consequences of Deliberate Self-Harm and Suicide Attempts." *Suicide and Life-Threatening Behavior* 37, no. 5 (2007): 543–52. https://doi.org/10.1521/suli.2007.37.5.543.

Chen, Hongtu, Elizabeth J. Kramer, Teddy Chen, and Henry Chung. "Engaging Asian Americans for Mental Health Research: Challenges and Solutions." *Journal of Immigrant Health* 7, no. 2 (2005): 109–18. https://doi.org/10.1007/s10903-005-2644-6.

Cho, Euiwan. "The Kingdom of God Is Big Enough for Both Collectivists and Individualists." *Fuller Magazine*, February 16, 2022. https://fullerstudio.fuller.edu/theology/the-kingdom-of-god-is-big-enough-for-both-collectivists-and-individualists/.

Coe, John H., and T. W. Hall. "A Transformational Psychology View." In Johnson, *Psychology and Christianity*.

Coleman, Monica A. *Bipolar Faith: A Black Woman's Journey with Depression and Faith*. Fortress, 2016.

Cooper-Chen, Anne, and Michiyo Tanaka. "Public Relations in Japan: The Cultural Roots of Kouhou." *Journal of Public Relations Research* 20, no. 1 (2007): 94–114. https://doi.org/10.1080/10627260701727036.

Crenshaw, Kimberlé. "Mapping the Margins: Intersectionality, Identity Politics, and Violence Against Women of Color." *Stanford Law Review* 43, no. 6 (1991): 1241–99. https://doi.org/10.2307/1229039.

Cross, William E., Jr. "The Negro-to-Black Conversion Experience: Toward a Psychology of Black Liberation." *Black World* 20, no. 9 (1971): 13–27.

Cuéllar, Israel, Bill Arnold, and Roberto Maldonado. "Acculturation Rating Scale for Mexican Americans-II: A Revision of the Original ARSMA Scale." *Hispanic Journal of Behavioral Sciences* 17, no. 3 (1995): 275–304. https://doi.org/10.1177/07399863950173001.

Curry, Jack. "Jealously Led Bonds to Steroids, Authors Say." *New York Times*, March 8, 2006. https://www.nytimes.com/2006/03/08/sports/baseball/jealousy-led-bonds-to-steroids-authors-say.html.

Davis, Don E., Joshua N. Hook, Everett L. Worthington et al. "Relational Humility: Conceptualizing and Measuring Humility as a Personality Judgment." *Journal of Personality Assessment* 93, no. 3 (2011): 225–34. https://doi.org/10.1080/00223891.2011.558871.

DeSouza, Flavia, Carmen Black Parker, E. Vanessa Spearman-McCarthy, Gina Newsome Duncan, and Reverend Maria Myers Black. "Coping with Racism: A Perspective of COVID-19 Church Closures on the Mental

Health of African Americans." *Journal of Racial and Ethnic Health Disparities* 8, no. 1 (2021): 7–11. https://doi.org/10.1007/s40615-020-00887-4.

De Vries, Wilco. "The Danger of Forcing Forgiveness." *Christianity Today*, May/June 2023. https://www.christianitytoday.com/2023/04/abuse-victims-danger-of-forced-forgiveness/.

Disney, Lindsey R. "Associations Between Humanitarianism, Othering, and Religious Affiliation." *Social Work and Christianity* 44, no. 3 (2017): 60–74.

Dottolo, Andrea L., and Abigail J. Stewart. "'I Never Think About My Race': Psychological Features of White Racial Identities." *Qualitative Research in Psychology* 10, no. 1 (2013): 102–17. https://doi.org/10.1080/14780887.2011.586449.

Dull, Brandon D., Leoandra Onnie Rogers, and Jade Ross. "Learning (Not) to Know: Examining How White Ignorance Manifests and Functions in White Adolescents' Racial Identity Narratives." *Child Development* 96, no. 3 (2025): 1000–1016. https://doi.org/10.1111/cdev.14215.

Eakin, Emily. "Bigotry as Mental Illness or Just Another Norm." *New York Times*, January 15, 2000. https://www.nytimes.com/2000/01/15/arts/bigotry-as-mental-illness-or-just-another-norm.html.

Eap, Sopagna, David S. DeGarmo, Ayaka Kawakami, Shelley N. Hara, Gordon C. N. Hall, and Andra L. Teten. "Culture and Personality Among European American and Asian American Men." *Journal of Cross-Cultural Psychology* 39, no. 5 (2008): 630–43. https://doi.org/10.1177/0022022108321310.

Edgar, William. *Created and Creating: A Biblical Theology of Culture*. InterVarsity, 2017.

Ekman, Paul, and Wallace V. Friesen. "Constants Across Cultures in the Face and Emotion." *Journal of Personality and Social Psychology* 17, no. 2 (1971): 124–29. https://doi.org/10.1037/h0030377.

Emerson, Michael O., and Christian Smith. *Divided by Faith: Evangelical Religion and the Problem of Race in America*. Oxford University Press, 2001.

Erikson, Erik H. *Childhood and Society*. Norton, 1963.

Ersahin, Zehra. "Post-Traumatic Growth Among Syrian Refugees in Turkey: The Role of Coping Strategies and Religiosity." *Current Psychology* 41, no. 4 (2022): 2398–407. https://doi.org/10.1007/s12144-020-00763-8.

Fix Team. "Transcript: The Third Democratic Debate." *Washington Post*, September 13, 2019. https://www.washingtonpost.com/politics/2019/09/13/transcript-third-democratic-debate/.

Gallagher-Thompson, Dolores, Lani S. Singer, Colin Depp, Brent T. Mausbach, Veronica Cardenas, and David W. Coon. "Effective Recruitment Strategies for Latino and Caucasian Dementia Family Caregivers in Intervention Research." *The American Journal of Geriatric Psychiatry* 12, no. 5 (2004): 484–90. https://doi.org/10.1097/00019442-200409000-00006.

Gambin, Malgorzata, and Carla Sharp. "The Relations Between Empathy, Guilt, Shame and Depression in Inpatient Adolescents." *Journal of Affective Disorders* 241 (2018): 381–87. https://doi.org/10.1016/j.jad.2018.08.068.

Gannon, Martin J., and Rajnandini Pillai. *Understanding Global Cultures: Metaphorical Journeys Through 31 Nations, Clusters of Nations, Continents, and Diversity*. 5th ed. Sage, 2013.

Gilbert, Paul. "The Relationship of Shame, Social Anxiety and Depression: The Role of the Evaluation of Social Rank." *Clinical Psychology and Psychotherapy* 7, no. 3 (2000): 174–89. https://doi.org/10.1002/1099-0879(200007)7:3<174::AID-CPP236>3.0.CO;2-U.

Gim Chung, Ruth H., Bryan S. K. Kim, and José M. Abreu. "Asian American Multidimensional Acculturation Scale: Development, Factor Analysis, Reliability, and Validity." *Cultural Diversity and Ethnic Minority Psychology* 10, no. 1 (2004): 66–80. https://doi.org/10.1037/1099-9809.10.1.66.

Gudykunst, William B., Yuko Matsumoto, Stella Ting-Toomey, Tsukasa Nishida, Kwangsu Kim, and Sam Heyman. "The Influence of Cultural Individualism-Collectivism, Self Construals, and Individual Values on Communication Styles Across Cultures." *Human Communication Research* 22, no. 4 (1996): 510–43. https://doi.org/10.1111/j.1468-2958.1996.tb00377.x.

Hall, Edward Twitchell. *Beyond Culture*. Anchor Books ed. Anchor Books, 1989.

Hamby, Sherry, "Know Thyself: How to Write a Reflexivity Statement," *Psychology Today*, May 22, 2018. https://www.psychologytoday.com/us/blog/the-web-of-violence/201805/know-thyself-how-to-write-a-reflexivity-statement.

Helms, Janet E., ed. *Black and White Racial Identity: Theory, Research, and Practice*. Greenwood, 1990.

Helms, Janet E. "Toward a Model of White Racial Identity Development." In *Black and White Racial Identity*.

Helms, Janet E. "An Update of Helm's White and People of Color Racial Identity Models." In *Handbook of Multicultural Counseling*, edited by

Joseph G. Ponterotto, J. Manuel Casas, Lisa A. Suzuki, and Charlene M. Alexander. Sage, 1995.

Hill, Daniel. *White Awake: An Honest Look at What It Means to Be White*. InterVarsity, 2017.

Holvino, Evangelina. "The 'Simultaneity' of Identities." In *New Perspectives on Racial Identity Development: Integrating Emerging Frameworks*, edited by Charmaine L. Wijeyesinghe and Bailey W. Jackon III. New York University Press, 2012.

Hong, Euny. *The Power of Nunchi: The Korean Secret to Happiness and Success*. Penguin Books, 2019.

Hong, Sehee, Bryan S. K. Kim, and Maren M. Wolfe. "A Psychometric Revision of the European American Values Scale for Asian Americans Using the Rasch Model." *Measurement and Evaluation in Counseling and Development* 37, no. 4 (2005): 194–207. https://doi.org/10.1080/07481756.2005.11909760.

Hook, Joshua N., and Don E. Davis. "Cultural Humility: Introduction to the Special Issue." *Journal of Psychology and Theology* 47, no. 2 (2019): 71–75. https://doi.org/10.1177/0091647119842410.

Horowitz, Juliana Menasce, Anna Brown, and Kiana Cox. *Race in America 2019*. Pew Research Center, April 9, 2019. https://www.pewresearch.org/wp-content/uploads/sites/20/2019/04/Race-report_updated-4.29.19.pdf.

Howell, Alan. "From 'Selves' to 'One Another': A Hospitable Proposal for a Post-Colonial Missions Paradigm of Interdependence." *Transformation: An International Journal of Holistic Mission Studies* 39, no. 3 (2022): 181–92. https://doi.org/10.1177/02653788221110780.

Hwang, John. *The Public Scholarship Manifesto*. Public Platform, accessed May 10, 2025. https://publicplatform.net/public-scholarship-manifesto/.

Ichimura, Emi, and Paul Youngbin Kim. "'Hope, but It's a Complex Kind': Reflections Following the War and Women's Human Rights Museum Visit; Part 1." *Christian Scholar's Review*, October 29, 2024. https://christianscholars.com/hope-but-its-a-complex-kind-reflections-following-the-war-and-womens-human-rights-museum-visit-part-1/.

Ichimura, Emi, and Paul Youngbin Kim. "'Hope, but It's a Complex Kind': Reflections Following the War and Women's Human Rights Museum Visit; Part 2." *Christian Scholar's Review*, October 29, 2024. https://christianscholars.com/hope-but-its-a-complex-kind-reflections-following-the-war-and-womens-human-rights-museum-visit-part-2/.

Johnson, Eric L. "A Brief History of Christians in Psychology." In Johnson, *Psychology and Christianity*.

Johnson, Eric L., ed. *Psychology and Christianity: Five Views*. 2nd ed. InterVarsity, 2010.

Jones, Stanton L. "An Integration View." In Johnson, *Psychology and Christianity*.

Kandemiri, Pride. "Forgiveness as a Positive Contributing Factor on the Mental Wellbeing of Congolese Refugees and Asylum Seekers Post-War Experience." *Journal of Human Behavior in the Social Environment* 29, no. 8 (2019): 1044–58. https://doi.org/10.1080/10911359.2019.1658685.

Kim, Bryan S. K. "Acculturation and Enculturation." In *Handbook of Asian American Psychology*, 2nd ed., edited by Frederick T. L. Leong, Arpana G. Inman, Angela Ebreo, Lawrence Hsin Yang, Lisa Kinoshita, and Michi Fu. Sage, 2007.

Kim, Bryan S. K., Lisa C. Li, and Gladys F. Ng. "The Asian American Values Scale–Multidimensional: Development, Reliability, and Validity." *Cultural Diversity and Ethnic Minority Psychology* 11, no. 3 (2005): 187–201. https://doi.org/10.1037/1099-9809.11.3.187.

Kim, Bryan S. K., and Michael M. Omizo. "Behavioral Acculturation and Enculturation and Psychological Functioning Among Asian American College Students." *Cultural Diversity and Ethnic Minority Psychology* 12, no. 2 (2006): 245–58. https://doi.org/10.1037/1099-9809.12.2.245.

Kim, Christina L., M. Elizabeth Lewis Hall, Tamara L. Anderson, and Michele M. Willingham. "Coping with Discrimination in Academia: Asian-American and Christian Perspectives." *Asian American Journal of Psychology* 2, no. 4 (2011): 291–305. https://doi.org/10.1037/a0025552.

Kim, Paul Youngbin. "'God Meant It for Good': Reflections on Meaning-Making." *Psychology Today*. June 28, 2023. https://www.psychologytoday.com/us/blog/culture-religion-and-psychology/202306/god-meant-it-for-good-reflections-on-meaning-making.

Kim, Paul Youngbin. "Korean Constructs of Nunchi, Jeong, and Han: Lessons for Interpersonal and Communal Flourishing." Unpublished manuscript, under review at *Christian Scholar's Review*, submitted April 19, 2025.

Kim, Paul Youngbin, host. "Racism and Total (with a Big T) Depravity: A Conversation with Dr. Alexander Jun." *Teaching Cross-Cultural Psychology*, podcast, April 12, 2024. https://www.youtube.com/watch?v=a5cWNKlrVtw.

Kim, Paul Youngbin. "Redeeming Korean Constructs of Han, Nunchi, and Jeong: Lessons for Interpersonal and Communal Flourishing." Winfred E. Weter Lectures, April 9, 2024, Seattle Pacific University, 1:29:02. https://digitalcommons.spu.edu/av_events/2852/.

Kim, Paul Youngbin. "Religious Support Mediates the Racial Microaggressions: Mental Health Relation Among Christian Ethnic Minority Students." *Psychology of Religion and Spirituality* 9, no. 2 (2017): 148–57. https://doi.org/10.1037/rel0000076.

Kim, Paul Youngbin. "Resisting the Allure of the Collectivism-Individualism Dichotomy in the Classroom: Han as an Example." *Christian Scholar's Review*, November 8, 2021. https://christianscholars.com/resisting-the-allure-of-the-collectivism-individualism-dichotomy-in-the-classroom-han-as-an-example/.

Kim, Paul Youngbin. "Revisiting and Extending the Role of Religious Coping in the Racism-Mental Health Relation Among Christian, Asian American Students." *Journal of Psychology and Theology* 45, no. 3 (2017): 166–81. https://doi.org/10.1177/009164711704500302.

Kim, Paul Youngbin. "A Tale of Two 'Tapes' in Public-Facing Scholarship: Gut Reactions and Helpful Reframes," *Christian Scholar's Review*, November 13, 2023. https://christianscholars.com/a-tale-of-two-tapes-in-public-facing-scholarship-gut-reactions-and-helpful-reframes/.

Kim, Paul Youngbin. "When My Own Students Microaggress Against Me." *Christian Scholar's Review*, September 12, 2023. https://christianscholars.com/when-my-own-students-microaggress-against-me/.

Kim, Paul Youngbin, Mika Govender, Katharine E. Bau, and Nicole V. Chiangpradit. "Racialized Experiences and Perspectives of International Students Enrolled in a Christian University: A Preliminary Qualitative Analysis." *International Journal of Christianity and Education* 29, no. 1 (2024). https://doi.org/10.1177/20569971241287201.

Kim, Paul Youngbin, Dana L. Kendall, and Katharine E. Bau. "Racial Microaggressions on Christian Campuses: Instrument Development and Exploratory Factor Analysis." *Christian Higher Education* 20, no. 5 (2021): 325–40. https://doi.org/10.1080/15363759.2020.1871120.

Kim, Paul Youngbin, Dana L. Kendall, and Hee-Sun Cheon. "Racial Microaggressions, Cultural Mistrust, and Mental Health Outcomes Among Asian American College Students." *American Journal of Orthopsychiatry* 87, no. 6 (2017): 663–70. https://doi.org/10.1037/ort0000203.

Kim, Paul Youngbin, Dana L. Kendall, and Marcia Webb. "Religious Coping Moderates the Relation Between Racism and Psychological

Well-Being Among Christian Asian American College Students." *Journal of Counseling Psychology* 62, no. 1 (2015): 87–94. https://doi.org/10.1037/cou0000055.

Kim, Paul Youngbin, Marcella A. Locke, Esal Shakil, Joo-Hwan Lee, and Nicole V. Chiangpradit. "Beliefs About Jesus's Race, Implicit Bias, and Cultural Correlates Among Asian American College Students." *Journal of Psychology and Theology* 51, no. 3 (2023): 333–51. https://doi.org/10.1177/00916471231161585.

Kim, Paul Youngbin, and Irene J. K. Park. "Testing a Multiple Mediation Model of Asian American College Students' Willingness to See a Counselor." *Cultural Diversity and Ethnic Minority Psychology* 15, no. 3 (2009): 295–302. https://doi.org/10.1037/a0014396.

Kim, Paul Youngbin, and Brittany M. Tausen. "White College Students' Ethnocultural Empathy Toward Asians and Asian Americans During the COVID-19 Pandemic." *Asian American Journal of Psychology* 13, no. 3 (2022): 305–13. https://doi.org/10.1037/aap0000246.

Kim, Sandra So Hee Chi. "Korean 'Han' and the Postcolonial Afterlives of 'The Beauty of Sorrow.'" *Korean Studies* 41 (2017): 253–79. http://www.jstor.org/stable/44508447.

Kirmayer, Laurence J. "Psychotherapy and the Cultural Concept of the Person." *Transcultural Psychiatry* 44, no. 2 (2007): 232–57. https://doi.org/10.1177/1363461506070794.

Kivel, Paul. *Uprooting Racism: How White People Can Work for Racial Justice*. 4th ed. New Society, 2017.

Knettel, Brandon A. "Attribution Through the Layperson's Lens: Development and Preliminary Validation of an Inclusive, International Measure of Beliefs About the Causes of Mental Illness." *Journal of Personality Assessment* 101, no. 1 (2019): 32–43. https://doi.org/10.1080/00223891.2017.1329738.

Koenig, Harold G., George R. Parkerson Jr., and Keith G. Meador. "Religion Index for Psychiatric Research." *American Journal of Psychiatry* 154, no. 6 (1997): 885–86. https://doi.org/10.1176/ajp.154.6.885b.

Koo, Katie, Ian Baker, and Jiyoon Yoon. "The First Year of Acculturation: A Longitudinal Study on Acculturative Stress and Adjustment Among the First Year International College Students." *Journal of International Students* 11, no. 2 (2021). https://doi.org/10.32674/jis.v11i2.1726.

Krua, Torli H. "Evangelism That Reconciles." In *No Longer Strangers: Transforming Evangelism with Immigrant Communities*, edited by Eugene Cho and Samira Izadi Page. Eerdmans, 2021.

Luhrmann, T. M., R. Padmavati, H. Tharoor, and A. Osei. "Differences in Voice-Hearing Experiences of People with Psychosis in the USA, India and Ghana: Interview-Based Study." *British Journal of Psychiatry* 206, no. 1 (2015): 41–44. https://doi.org/10.1192/bjp.bp.113.139048.

Lynn, Monty L., Michael J. Naughton, and Steve VanderVeen. "Faith at Work Scale (FWS): Justification, Development, and Validation of a Measure of Judaeo-Christian Religion in the Workplace." *Journal of Business Ethics* 85, no. 2 (2009): 227–43. https://doi.org/10.1007/s10551-008-9767-3.

Marcia, James E. "Identity in Adolescence." In *Handbook of Adolescent Psychology*, edited by Joseph Adelson. Wiley & Sons, 1980.

Markus, Hazel R., and Shinobu Kitayama. "Culture and the Self: Implications for Cognition, Emotion, and Motivation." *Psychological Review* 98, no. 2 (1991): 224–53. https://doi.org/10.1037/0033-295X.98.2.224.

Marroquín, Brett, Howard Tennen, and Annette L. Stanton. "Coping, Emotion Regulation, and Well-Being: Intrapersonal and Interpersonal Processes." In *The Happy Mind: Cognitive Contributions to Well-Being*, edited by Michael D. Robinson and Michael Eid. Springer International, 2017. https://doi.org/10.1007/978-3-319-58763-9_14.

Matos, Lisa, Pedro A. Costa, Crystal L. Park, Monica J. Indart, and Isabel Leal. "'The War Made Me a Better Person': Syrian Refugees' Meaning-Making Trajectories in the Aftermath of Collective Trauma." *International Journal of Environmental Research and Public Health* 18, no. 16 (2021). https://doi.org/10.3390/ijerph18168481.

Matsumoto, David, and Linda Juang. *Culture and Psychology*. 6th ed. Cengage Learning, 2017.

Matsumoto, David, and Caroline Anne Leong Jones. "Ethical Issues in Cross-Cultural Psychology." In *The Handbook of Social Research Ethics*, by Donna Mertens and Pauline Ginsberg, 323–36. Sage, 2009. https://doi.org/10.4135/9781483348971.n21.

McCaulley, Esau. *Reading While Black: African American Biblical Interpretation as an Exercise in Hope*. IVP Academic, 2020.

McConnell, John M., Vincent Bacote, Edward B. Davis et al. "Including Multiculturalism, Social Justice, and Peace Within the Integration of Psychology and Theology: Barriers and a Call to Action." *Journal of Psychology and Theology* 49, no. 1 (2020): 5–21. https://doi.org/10.1177/0091647120974989.

Mehta, Sharan Kaur, Rachel C. Schneider, and Elaine Howard Ecklund. "'God Sees No Color' so Why Should I? How White Christians Produce

Divinized Colorblindness." *Sociological Inquiry* 92, no. 2 (2022): 623–46. https://doi.org/10.1111/soin.12476.

Meinert, J. A. "Bridging the Gap: Recruitment of African-American Women into Mental Health Research Studies." *Academic Psychiatry* 27, no. 1 (2003): 21–28. https://doi.org/10.1176/appi.ap.27.1.21.

Miller, Matthew J. "A Bilinear Multidimensional Measurement Model of Asian American Acculturation and Enculturation: Implications for Counseling Interventions." *Journal of Counseling Psychology* 54, no. 2 (2007): 118–31. https://doi.org/10.1037/0022-0167.54.2.118.

Mio, Jeffery Scott, Lori A. Barker, Melanie M. Domenech Rodríguez, and John Gonzalez. *Multicultural Psychology: Understanding Our Diverse Communities*. 6th ed. Oxford University Press, 2023.

Moriarty, Morgan. "Sean McVay Has a Get-Back Coach: Clemson's Pioneering Get-Back Coach Explains the Job." SBNation.com, February 2, 2019. https://www.sbnation.com/nfl/2019/2/2/18191956/sean-mcvay-get-back-coach-rams-clemson.

Muraya, Julie Gathoni, Ann Neville Miller, and Leonard Mjomba. "Implications of High-/Low-Context Communication for Target Audience Member Interpretation of Messages in the *Nimechill* Abstinence Campaign in Nairobi, Kenya." *Health Communication* 26, no. 6 (2011): 516–24. https://doi.org/10.1080/10410236.2011.556083.

Muruthi, Bertranna A., Savannah S. Young, Jessica Chou, Emily Janes, and Maliha Ibrahim. "'We Pray as a Family': The Role of Religion for Resettled Karen Refugees." *Journal of Family Issues* 41, no. 10 (2020): 1723–41. https://doi.org/10.1177/0192513X20911068.

Myers, David G. "A Levels-of-Explanation View." In Johnson, *Psychology and Christianity*.

Myers, David G. "Steering Between the Extremes: On Being a Christian Scholar in Psychology." *Christian Scholar's Review* 20 (1991): 376–83.

Myers, David G., and Malcolm A. Jeeves. *Psychology Through the Eyes of Faith*. Rev. ed. HarperSanFrancisco, 2003.

Naufel, Karen Z., Drew C. Appleby, Jason Young et al. "The Skillful Psychology Student: Prepared for Success in the 21st Century Workplace." American Psychological Association, 2019. www.apa.org/careers/resources/guides/transferable-skills.pdf.

Neville, Helen A., and Alex L. Pieterse. "Racism, White Supremacy, and Resistance: Contextualizing Black American Experiences." In *Handbook of African American Psychology*, edited by Helen A. Neville, Brendesha M. Tynes, and Shawn O. Utsey. Sage, 2009.

Nguyen, Angela-MinhTu D., and Verónica Benet-Martínez. "Biculturalism and Adjustment: A Meta-Analysis." *Journal of Cross-Cultural Psychology* 44, no. 1 (2013): 122–59. https://doi.org/10.1177/0022022111435097.

Ochu, Austin C., Edward B. Davis, Gina Magyar-Russell, Kari A. O'Grady, and Jamie D. Aten. "Religious Coping, Dispositional Forgiveness, and Posttraumatic Outcomes in Adult Survivors of the Liberian Civil War." *Spirituality in Clinical Practice* 5, no. 2 (2018): 104–19. https://doi.org/10.1037/scp0000163.

Pargament, Kenneth I. *The Psychology of Religion and Coping: Theory, Research, Practice*. Guilford, 1997.

Pargament, Kenneth I., Margaret Feuille, and Donna Burdzy. "The Brief RCOPE: Current Psychometric Status of a Short Measure of Religious Coping." *Religions* 2, no. 1 (2011): 51–76. https://doi.org/10.3390/rel2010051.

Pargament, Kenneth I., Harold G. Koenig, and Lisa M. Perez. "The Many Methods of Religious Coping: Development and Initial Validation of the RCOPE." *Journal of Clinical Psychology* 56, no. 4 (2000): 519–43. https://doi.org/10.1002/(SICI)1097-4679(200004)56:4<519::AID-JCLP6>3.0.CO;2-1.

Parham, Thomas A. "Cycles of Psychological Nigrescence." *The Counseling Psychologist* 17, no. 2 (1989): 187–226. https://doi.org/10.1177/0011000089172001.

Park, Crystal L. "Making Sense of the Meaning Literature: An Integrative Review of Meaning Making and Its Effects on Adjustment to Stressful Life Events." *Psychological Bulletin* 136, no. 2 (2010): 257–301. https://doi.org/10.1037/a0018301.

Park, Hee Sun, Timothy R. Levine, Rene Weber et al. "Individual and Cultural Variations in Direct Communication Style." *International Journal of Intercultural Relations* 36, no. 2 (2012): 179–87. https://doi.org/10.1016/j.ijintrel.2011.12.010.

Park, Yong S., and Bryan S. K. Kim. "Asian and European American Cultural Values and Communication Styles Among Asian American and European American College Students." *Cultural Diversity and Ethnic Minority Psychology* 14, no. 1 (2008): 47–56. https://doi.org/10.1037/1099-9809.14.1.47.

Parker, G., Y.-C. Cheah, and K. Roy. "Do the Chinese Somatize Depression? A Cross-Cultural Study." *Social Psychiatry and Psychiatric Epidemiology* 36, no. 6 (2001): 287–93. https://doi.org/10.1007/s001270170046.

Pettigrew, Thomas F. "Ethnocentrism." In *Encyclopedia of Social Measurement*, edited by Kimberly Kempf-Leonard. Elsevier, 2005. https://doi.org/10.1016/B0-12-369398-5/00194-8.

Philip, Selin, Anita A. Neuer Colburn, Lee Underwood, and Hannah Bayne. "The Impact of Religion/Spirituality on Acculturative Stress Among International Students." *Journal of College Counseling* 22, no. 1 (2019): 27–40. https://doi.org/10.1002/jocc.12112.

Phinney, Jean S. "The Multigroup Ethnic Identity Measure: A New Scale for Use with Diverse Groups." *Journal of Adolescent Research* 7, no. 2 (1992): 156–76. https://doi.org/10.1177/074355489272003.

Phinney, Jean S. "Stages of Ethnic Identity Development in Minority Group Adolescents." *The Journal of Early Adolescence* 9, nos. 1–2 (1989): 34–49. https://doi.org/10.1177/0272431689091004.

Phinney, Jean S., and Anthony D. Ong. "Conceptualization and Measurement of Ethnic Identity: Current Status and Future Directions." *Journal of Counseling Psychology* 54, no. 3 (2007): 271–81. https://doi.org/10.1037/0022-0167.54.3.271.

Powell, Wizdom, Kira Hudson Banks, and Jacqueline S. Mattis. "Buried Hatchets, Marked Locations: Forgiveness, Everyday Racial Discrimination, and African American Men's Depressive Symptomatology." *American Journal of Orthopsychiatry* 87, no. 6 (2017): 646–62. https://doi.org/10.1037/ort0000210.

Powlison, David. "A Biblical Counseling View." In Johnson, *Psychology and Christianity*.

Quinton, Wendy J. "Unwelcome on Campus? Predictors of Prejudice Against International Students." *Journal of Diversity in Higher Education* 12, no. 2 (2019): 156–69. https://doi.org/10.1037/dhe0000091.

Redfield, Robert, Ralph Linton, and Melville J. Herskovits. "Memorandum for the Study of Acculturation." *American Anthropologist* 38, no. 1 (1936): 149–52. http://www.jstor.org/stable/662563.

Roberts, Robert C., and P. J. Watson. "A Christian Psychology View." In Johnson, *Psychology and Christianity*.

Rogers, Carl R. *Client-Centered Therapy: Its Current Practice, Implications, and Theory*. Houghton Mifflin, 1965.

Rogers, Carl R. *On Becoming a Person: A Therapist's View of Psychotherapy*. Houghton Mifflin, 1989.

Roosa, Mark W., George P. Knight, and Adriana J. Umaña-Taylor. "Research with Underresearched Populations." In *APA Handbook of Research Methods in Psychology*, edited by Harris Cooper. Vol. 1, *Foundations, Planning, Measures, and Psychometrics*, edited by Harris Cooper, Paul M. Camic, Debra L. Long, A. T. Panter, David Rindskopf, and Kenneth J. Sher. American Psychological Association, 2012. https://doi.org/10.1037/13619-007.

Roser, Max. "The Map We Need If We Want to Think About How Global Living Conditions Are Changing." Our World in Data, September 12, 2018. https://ourworldindata.org/world-population-cartogram.

Rothwell, Robert. "What Is TULIP?" Ligonier, August 30, 2021. https://www.ligonier.org/learn/articles/what-tulip.

Rowatt, Wade C., Rosemary L. Al-Kire, Hilary Dunn, and Joseph Leman. "Attitudes Toward Separating Immigrant Families at the United States–Mexico Border." *Analyses of Social Issues and Public Policy* 20, no. 1 (2020): 118–42. https://doi.org/10.1111/asap.12198.

Rowe, Wayne, Sandra K. Bennett, and Donald R. Atkinson. "White Racial Identity Models: A Critique and Alternative Proposal." *The Counseling Psychologist* 22, no. 1 (1994): 129–46. https://doi.org/10.1177/0011000094221009.

Salifu Yendork, Joana, Gladys Beryl Brew, Elizabeth A. Sarfo, and Lily Kpobi. "Mental Illness Has Multiple Causes: Beliefs on Causes of Mental Illness by Congregants of Selected Neo-Prophetic Churches in Ghana." *Mental Health, Religion and Culture* 21, no. 7 (2018): 647–66. https://doi.org/10.1080/13674676.2018.1511694.

Sandhu, Daya S., and Badiolah R. Asrabadi. "Development of an Acculturative Stress Scale for International Students: Preliminary Findings." *Psychological Reports* 75, no. 1 (1994): 435–48. https://doi.org/10.2466/pr0.1994.75.1.435.

Schinkel, Sanne, Barbara C. Schouten, Fatmagül Kerpiclik, Bas Van Den Putte, and Julia C. M. Van Weert. "Perceptions of Barriers to Patient Participation: Are They Due to Language, Culture, or Discrimination?" *Health Communication* 34, no. 12 (2019): 1469–81. https://doi.org/10.1080/10410236.2018.1500431.

Singelis, Theodore M. "The Measurement of Independent and Interdependent Self-Construals." *Personality and Social Psychology Bulletin* 20, no. 5 (1994): 580–91. https://doi.org/10.1177/0146167294205014.

Stangor, Charles. "The Study of Stereotyping, Prejudice, and Discrimination Within Social Psychology: A Quick History of Theory and Research." In *Handbook of Prejudice, Stereotyping, and Discrimination*, edited by Todd. D. Nelson. Taylor & Francis Group, 2009.

Stearns, Rich. "Blessed by a Broken Heart." World Vision, last updated August 28, 2017. https://www.worldvision.org/hunger-news-stories/blessed-broken-heart.

Sue, Derald Wing. "Microaggressions and 'Evidence': Empirical or Experiential Reality?" *Perspectives on Psychological Science* 12, no. 1 (2017): 170–72. https://doi.org/10.1177/1745691616664437.

Sue, Derald Wing, Sarah Alsaidi, Michael N. Awad, Elizabeth Glaeser, Cassandra Z. Calle, and Narolyn Mendez. "Disarming Racial Microaggressions: Microintervention Strategies for Targets, White Allies, and Bystanders." *American Psychologist* 74, no. 1 (2019): 128–42. https://doi.org/10.1037/amp0000296.

Sue, Derald Wing, Patricia Arredondo, and Roderick J. McDavis. "Multicultural Counseling Competencies and Standards: A Call to the Profession." *Journal of Counseling and Development* 70, no. 4 (1992): 477–86. https://doi.org/10.1002/j.1556-6676.1992.tb01642.x.

Sue, Derald Wing, Christina M. Capodilupo, Gina C. Torino et al. "Racial Microaggressions in Everyday Life: Implications for Clinical Practice." *American Psychologist* 62, no. 4 (2007): 271–86. https://doi.org/10.1037/0003-066x.62.4.271.

Sue, Derald Wing, and David Sue. *Counseling the Culturally Different: Theory and Practice*. 2nd ed. Wiley & Sons, 1990.

Sue, Derald Wing, and David Sue. *Counseling the Culturally Different: Theory and Practice*. 3rd ed. Wiley & Sons, 1999.

Sue, Derald Wing, and David Sue. "Racial/Cultural Identity Development in People of Color: Counseling Implications." In *Counseling the Culturally Diverse: Theory and Practice*. 7th ed. Wiley & Sons, 2016.

Sue, Stanley. "Science, Ethnicity, and Bias: Where Have We Gone Wrong?" *American Psychologist* 54, no. 12 (1999): 1070–77. https://doi.org/10.1037/0003-066X.54.12.1070.

Szymanski, Dawn M., and Oluwafunmilayo Obiri. "Do Religious Coping Styles Moderate or Mediate the External and Internalized Racism-Distress Links?" *The Counseling Psychologist* 39, no. 3 (2011): 438–62. https://doi.org/10.1177/0011000010378895.

Tajfel, Henri, and John Turner. "An Integrative Theory of Intergroup Conflict." In *The Social Psychology of Intergroup Relations*, edited by William G. Austin and Stephen Worchel. Brooks/Cole, 1979.

Tajfel, Henri, and John Turner. "The Social Identity Theory of Intergroup Behavior." In *Psychology of Intergroup Relations*, edited by William G. Austin and Stephen Worchel. Nelson Hall, 1986.

Tan, Siang-Yang. *Counseling and Psychotherapy: A Christian Perspective*. 2nd ed. Baker Academic, 2022.

Tatum, Beverly Daniel. *"Why Are All the Black Kids Sitting Together in the Cafeteria?": And Other Conversations About Race*. 3rd ed. Basic Books, 2017.

Taylor, Steve, Divine Charura, Glenn Williams et al. "Loss, Grief, and Growth: An Interpretative Phenomenological Analysis of Experiences of Trauma in Asylum Seekers and Refugees." *Traumatology* 30, no. 1 (2024): 103–12. https://doi.org/10.1037/trm0000250.

Tedeschi, Richard G., and Lawrence G. Calhoun. "The Posttraumatic Growth Inventory: Measuring the Positive Legacy of Trauma." *Journal of Traumatic Stress* 9, no. 3 (1996): 455–71. https://doi.org/10.1002/jts.2490090305.

Thalmayer, Amber Gayle, Cecilia Toscanelli, and Jeffrey Jensen Arnett. "The Neglected 95% Revisited: Is American Psychology Becoming Less American?" *American Psychologist* 76, no. 1 (2021): 116–29. https://doi.org/10.1037/amp0000622.

Tisby, Jemar. *The Color of Compromise: The Truth About the American Church's Complicity in Racism*. Zondervan Reflective, 2019.

Triandis, Harry C. *The Analysis of Subjective Culture*. Comparative Studies in Behavioral Science. Wiley-Interscience, 1972.

Triandis, Harry C., Robert Bontempo, Marcelo J. Villareal, Masaaki Asai, and Nydia Lucca. "Individualism and Collectivism: Cross-Cultural Perspectives on Self-Ingroup Relationships." *Journal of Personality and Social Psychology* 54, no. 2 (1988): 323–38. https://doi.org/10.1037/0022-3514.54.2.323.

Triandis, Harry C., and Michele J. Gelfand. "Converging Measurement of Horizontal and Vertical Individualism and Collectivism." *Journal of Personality and Social Psychology* 74, no. 1 (1998): 118–28. https://doi.org/10.1037/0022-3514.74.1.118.

Vazquez, Veola E., Joshua J. Knabb, Charles Lee-Johnson, and Krystal Hays. *Healing Conversations on Race: Four Key Practices from Scripture and Psychology*. IVP Academic, 2023.

Vazquez, Veola E., Jaimee Stutz-Johnson, and Roy Sorbel. "Black-White Biracial Christians, Discrimination, and Mental Health: A Moderated Mediation Model of Church Support and Religious Coping." *Psychology of Religion and Spirituality* 15, no. 1 (2023): 6–17. https://doi.org/10.1037/rel0000415.

Vogel, David L., Haley A. Strass, Patrick J. Heath et al. "Stigma of Seeking Psychological Services: Examining College Students Across Ten Countries/Regions." *The Counseling Psychologist* 45, no. 2 (2017): 170–92. https://doi.org/10.1177/0011000016671411.

Wallace, Phyllis M., Elizabeth A. Pomery, Amy E. Latimer, Josefa L. Martinez, and Peter Salovey. "A Review of Acculturation Measures and Their Utility in Studies Promoting Latino Health." *Hispanic Journal of Behavioral Sciences* 32, no. 1 (2010): 37–54. https://doi.org/10.1177/0739986309352341.

Wallis, Jim. *America's Original Sin: Racism, White Privilege, and the Bridge to a New America*. Brazos, 2017.

Wang, Alton. "The Downside of Andrew Yang's Jokes About Knowing Lots of Asian American Doctors." *Washington Post*, September 16, 2019. https://www.washingtonpost.com/outlook/2019/09/16/downside-andrew-yangs-jokes-about-knowing-lots-asian-american-doctors/.

Wang, Yu-Wei, M. Meghan Davidson, Oksana F. Yakushko, Holly Bielstein Savoy, Jeffrey A. Tan, and Joseph K. Bleier. "The Scale of Ethnocultural Empathy: Development, Validation, and Reliability." *Journal of Counseling Psychology* 50, no. 2 (2003): 221–34. https://doi.org/10.1037/0022-0167.50.2.221.

Westermeyer, Joseph. "Cultural Factors in Clinical Assessment." *Journal of Consulting and Clinical Psychology* 55, no. 4 (1987): 471–78. https://doi.org/10.1037/0022-006X.55.4.471.

Williams, Marlene G., and Jioni A. Lewis. "Gendered Racial Microaggressions and Depressive Symptoms Among Black Women: A Moderated Mediation Model." *Psychology of Women Quarterly* 43, no. 3 (2019): 368–80. https://doi.org/10.1177/0361684319832511.

Wilson, Jessie, Colleen Ward, Velichko H. Fetvadjiev, and Alicia Bethel. "Measuring Cultural Competencies: The Development and Validation of a Revised Measure of Sociocultural Adaptation." *Journal of*

Cross-Cultural Psychology 48, no. 10 (2017): 1475–506. https://doi.org/10.1177/0022022117732721.

Wolterstorff, Nicholas. “You Need Two Eyes.” Lecture, May 20, 2006, Calvin College. https://digitalcommons.calvin.edu/other_lectures/1/.

Wong, Y. Joel, Shu-Yi Wang, and Elyssa M. Klann. “The Emperor with No Clothes: A Critique of Collectivism and Individualism.” *Archives of Scientific Psychology* 6, no. 1 (2018): 251–60. https://doi.org/10.1037/arc0000059.

Worthington, Everett L., Nathaniel G. Wade, Terry L. Hight et al. “The Religious Commitment Inventory—10: Development, Refinement, and Validation of a Brief Scale for Research and Counseling.” *Journal of Counseling Psychology* 50, no. 1 (2003): 84–96. https://doi.org/10.1037/0022-0167.50.1.84.

Würtz, Elizabeth. “Intercultural Communication on Web Sites: A Cross-Cultural Analysis of Web Sites from High-Context Cultures and Low-Context Cultures.” *Journal of Computer-Mediated Communication* 11, no. 1 (November 2005): 274–99. https://doi.org/10.1111/j.1083-6101.2006.tb00313.x.

Yantis, Caitlyn. “The Role of White Identity in Anti-Racist Allyship.” *Social and Personality Psychology Compass* 18, no. 9 (2024): 1–15. https://doi.org/10.1111/spc3.70005.

Yellow Horse, Aggie J., Russell Jeung, and Ronae Matriano. *Stop AAPI Hate National Report: March 19, 2020–September 30, 2021*. Stop AAPI Hate, 2021. https://stopaapihate.org/wp-content/uploads/2021/11/21-SAH-NationalReport2-v2.pdf.

Yoo, Hyung Chol, Kimberly S. Burrola, and Michael F. Steger. “A Preliminary Report on a New Measure: Internalization of the Model Minority Myth Measure (IM-4) and Its Psychological Correlates Among Asian American College Students.” *Journal of Counseling Psychology* 57, no. 1 (2010): 114–27. https://doi.org/10.1037/a0017871.

Yoon, Eunju, Latifat Cabirou, Sarah Galvin et al. “A Meta-Analysis of Acculturation and Enculturation: Bilinear, Multidimensional, and Context-Dependent Processes.” *The Counseling Psychologist* 48, no. 3 (2020): 342–76. https://doi.org/10.1177/0011000019898583.

Yoon, Hanha. “How to Respond to Microaggressions.” *New York Times*, March 3, 2020. https://www.nytimes.com/2020/03/03/smarter-living/how-to-respond-to-microaggressions.html.

Zane, Nolan, and May Yeh. “The Use of Culturally-Based Variables in Assessment: Studies on Loss of Face.” In *Asian American Mental Health*, edited by Karen S. Kurasaki, Sumie Okazaki, and Stanley Sue. Springer US, 2002. https://doi.org/10.1007/978-1-4615-0735-2_9.

Zhu, Liwei. "Personal Mental Impacts of Christian Faith in Cross-Cultural Adaptation of Chinese Migrants in Ireland." *Mental Health, Religion and Culture* 25, no. 4 (2022): 448–61. https://doi.org/10.1080/13674676.2022.2028749.

Index